Antilogophoricity and Binding Theory

Antilogophoricity and Binding Theory

Jun Yashima

KAITAKUSHA

Kaitakusha Co., Ltd.
5-2, Mukogaoka 1-chome
Bunkyo-ku, Tokyo 113-0023
Japan

Antilogophoricity and Binding Theory

Published in Japan
by Kaitakusha Co., Ltd., Tokyo

Copyright © 2016
by Jun Yashima

All rights reserved. No part of this publication may be reproduced, stored in a retrieval system, or transmitted, in any form or by any means, electronic, mechanical, photocopying, recording, or otherwise, without the prior permission of the copyright owner.

First published 2016

Printed and bound in Japan
by ARM Corporation

Cover design by Shihoko Nakamura

Preface

This book is a revised version of my Ph.D. dissertation (entitled *Antilogophoricity: In conspiracy with the Binding Theory*), submitted to the Department of Linguistics at the University of California, Los Angeles in 2015.

Since I believe that the basic ideas and findings presented in the dissertation are still valid and important both empirically and theoretically, I have kept as much of the original content as possible. For this reason, the revisions that have been made are primarily of a minor nature (such as correcting typographical errors and updating references).

As this book grew out of my dissertation, I would first and foremost like to express my profound gratitude to those who have helped me bring my dissertation to completion.

My greatest thanks go to Dominique Sportiche for his guidance, encouragement, and support. Many of the ideas presented in this work evolved from discussions with Dominique. Had he not bombarded me with so many Socratic questions, my dissertation would have been completed much earlier but would have been of far less quality.

I'm also grateful to the other members of my Ph.D. committee. Hilda Koopman is the primary reason that I decided to pursue a Ph.D. at UCLA. I've been mesmerized and spellbound by the phenomenal way in which she motivates iconoclastic ideas. I've learned from her how to think outside the box.

Nina Hyams kindled my interest in language acquisition. I hadn't received any formal education on language acquisition until I took her graduate course on grammatical development. I worked on several acquisition-related projects during my years at UCLA, and I owe a tremendous debt to her for her input.

As an external member, Mamoru Saito meticulously read a draft of my dissertation and gave me detailed comments, from which I greatly benefited. I'm also more than grateful to him for coming to my dissertation defense all the way from Japan.

Vincent Homer, the other external member, served as my de-facto advisor while I was in Paris. His suggestions and comments helped shape the ideas presented in this work. Definitely, he's gone way beyond the call of duty.

Other professors at UCLA inspired me at various stages of my graduate studies. I extend my gratitude, in particular, to Ed Keenan, Anoop Mahajan, Yael Sharvit, Tim Stowell, and Carson Schütze.

Many thanks also go to my fellow graduate students at UCLA for making my Ph.D. journey fulfilling and memorable: Natasha Abner, Byron Ahn, Nikos Angelopoulos, Jason Bishop, Dustin Bowers, Joe Buffington, Isabelle Charnavel, Philippe Côté-Boucher, Meaghan Fowlie, John Gluckman, Thomas Graf, Yuhi Inoue, Yun Jung Kim, Natasha Korotkova, Michael Lefkowitz, Sadie Martin, Kathleen O'Flynn, Craig Sailor, Yu Tanaka, and Lauren Winans.

For helping with data collection, I'm indebted to Malone Dunlavy, Edward Nguyen, and Frank Staniszewski.

I also want to express my heartfelt gratitude to Takane Ito, Kunio Nishiyama, Reiko Okabe, Natsumi Shibata, Yasutada Sudo, and Akira Watanabe, without whose help I couldn't have even started my Ph.D. at UCLA.

Chapter 3 is an extended version of Yashima (2015) ("On the apparent unbindability of overt third-person pronouns in Japanese" in *Natural Language and Linguistic Theory* 33, 1421–1438).

My graduate research was supported in part by a Fulbright grant.

Table of Contents

Preface v
List of Tables x
List of Abbreviations x

Chapter 1   Overview of this Book 1

Chapter 2   Between the Binding Theory and Logophoricity 9
  2.1. Binding Theory 9
  2.2. Challenges to the Binding Theory 18
  2.3. Logophoricity 24
      2.3.1. Logophoric Domains 25
          2.3.1.1. Logophoric Domain 1: Complement Clauses of Verbs of Speech 25
          2.3.1.2. Logophoric Domain 2: Complements of Verbs of Thought, Psychological State and Perception 26
          2.3.1.3. Logophoric Domain 3: Adverbial Clauses 27
          2.3.1.4. Logophoric Domain 4: Relative Clauses 31
          2.3.1.5. Logophoric Domain 5: Simple Clauses 33
      2.3.2. Logocentric Antecedents 35

2.4. Antilogophoricity ·· 40
2.5. Binding vs. Coreference (Covaluation) ·· 41

Chapter 3 Concealed Antilogophoricity: A Case Study of Japanese Pronominal Binding ·· 47
3.1. Overt third-person pronouns in Japanese ··· 47
3.2. Basic Facts ·· 50
3.3. The (Putative) "Unbindability" of Overt Third-Person Pronouns: Previous Studies ·· 53
   3.3.1. Sportiche (1986) ·· 53
   3.3.2. Aoun and Hornstein (1992) and Katada (1991) ····························· 56
   3.3.3. Montalbetti (1984) ··· 60
   3.3.4. Japanese Third-Person Pronouns as NPs (Kuroda 1965) ·············· 62
   3.3.5. Japanese Pronouns as N-Pronouns (Noguchi 1995, 1997; Déchaine and Wiltschko 2002) ·· 66
   3.3.6. Japanese Personal Pronouns Are Not NPs ·································· 69
   3.3.7. Japanese Third-Person Pronouns as Demonstratives (Kitagawa 1981; Hoji 1990, 1991) ··· 72
3.4. The "Bindability" of Overt Third-Person Pronouns: Previous Studies ·· 76
   3.4.1. Hoji et al. (2000) ·· 76
   3.4.2. Hara (2002) ·· 80
3.5. The Antilogophoricity Account ·· 84
   3.5.1. Epithets and Antilogophoricity ·· 84
   3.5.2. Japanese Overt Third-Person Pronouns as Epithets ···················· 91
   3.5.3. The Apparent Absence of Antilogophoric Effects ·························· 96
3.6. Summary of the Chapter and Remaining Issues ······································· 101

Chapter 4 Antilogophoricity and the Scope of Condition C ······························· 105
4.1. Condition C and Antilogophoricity ··· 105
4.2. Names as Maximal Antilogophors ··· 112
4.3. *Zibun* as a Tool for Locating Potential Logocentric Antecedents ··· 117
4.4. The Scope of Condition C ·· 122

    4.4.1. Condition C Revisited 122
    4.4.2. Intervention Effects 125
  4.5. Summary 137

Chapter 5 Conclusion 139

References 143

Index 151

List of Tables

Table 2.1   Types of Logophoricity 37
Table 3.1   Nominal Proform Typology (Déchaine and Wiltschko
            2002: 410) 67
Table 3.2   Deictic Demonstratives in Japanese 73

List of Abbreviations

ACC = accusative case
ADES = adessive postposition
ASP = aspect
AUX = auxiliary
BEN = benefactive postposition
CL = classifier
COMP = complementizer
COP = copula
DAT = dative case
DEF = definite
DUR = durative
EMP = empathy marker
EMPH = emphatics
F1 = future today
GEN = genitive case
HAB = habitual aspect
HON = honorific marker
IMPF = imperfective
IND = indicative mood
LDA = long-distance anaphora
LOC = locative
LOG = logophoric form/pronoun
NEG = negation
NOM = nominative case

O = object
PART = particle
PASS = passive
PAST = past tense
PERF = perfective
PFAT = perfective absolute transitive
Pl = plural
POSS = possessive
PRES = present tense
Pro = pronoun
PROG = progressive
Q = question particle
RED = reduplication
REL = relative clause marker
SBJ = subjective mood
SBRD = subordinator
SG = singular
SGM = singular male
SP = speaker
STAT = stative aspect
TOP = topic
1 = first person
3 = third person

Chapter 1

Overview of this Book

One of the recurring issues in the formulation of the Binding Theory is concerned with variation in anaphoric patterns.[1] Since the very inception of the theory it has been observed that within and across languages, nominal expressions that seemingly belong to the same class do not always behave in exactly the same manner. For years attempts have been made to make the theory flexible enough to accommodate the attested patterns, while at the same time keeping it sufficiently restrictive to prevent overgeneration.

Within the framework of generative grammar, three approaches have figured prominently in the discussion of variation in binding systems. One approach that crystallized in the Principles-and-Parameters era is to hypothesize that certain components of the Binding Theory (in particular, the way locality is computed) allow for parametric variation (Anderson 1986; Manzini and Wexler 1987, *inter alia*). For example, Aoun and Hornstein (1992) propose that Condition B is composed of two separate disjoint-reference requirements: one that disallows A-binding of a pronoun in some specified domain, and one that disallows A'-binding in some specified domain. They claim that in English, these two disjointness conditions happen to apply in the same domain, but some languages impose them on separate domains. In

---

[1] The interested reader is referred to Freidin (1992), who offers a concise overview of crosslinguistic differences in binding domains.

a similar vein, Lasnik (1989) argues that Condition C splits into two conditions, one of which is subject to parametric variation (see also Narahara 1991).

Another line of approach is to attribute superficial differences to movement operations, instead of parameterizing the binding domain per se (Pica 1987; Battistella 1989, *inter alia*). For instance, Pica (1987) argues that morphologically simplex anaphors undergo LF movement to INFL, where they can get locally bound by their antecedent. On this view, certain properties of long-distance anaphoric dependencies are claimed to follow from general constraints on movement.

Still another approach is to claim that prima facie violations of the Binding Theory are somehow "exempt" from the relevant conditions (Reinhart and Reuland 1991, 1993; Pollard and Sag 1992, *inter alia*). Long-distance anaphors are a case in point. For example, it has been claimed by some researchers that long-distance anaphors such as the Japanese reflexive *zibun* are, in fact, logophoric pronouns, which are not subject to structural conditions in the syntax but are presumably regulated by certain discourse conditions (Kuno 1978; Kameyama 1985; Sells 1987a, among others). On this view, long-distance anaphors do not fall under Condition A, and as such do not constitute a counterexample to the Binding Theory.

There is substantial empirical support for the third approach. Again, take long-distance anaphors for example. It has been reported that unlike local anaphors, long-distance anaphors can take a non-c-commanding antecedent. (Here I gloss a long-distance anaphor as LDA.)

(1) Icelandic
 Skoðun Siggu$_1$ er að sig$_1$ vanti hæfileika.
 opinion Sigga's is that LDA lacks talent
 'Sigga$_1$'s opinion is that she$_1$ lacks talent.'

(Maling 1984: 222)

(2) Japanese
 Zibun$_1$-ga baka-na koto-ga Taroo$_1$-o kanasimaseta.
 LDA-NOM fool-COP COMP-NOM Taro-ACC saddened
 'That he$_1$ was a fool saddened Taro$_1$.'

(Kuno 1978: 194)

In (1)–(2), the antecedent of the long-distance anaphor does not appear to sit in a position c-commanding the anaphor, but binding is nevertheless possible.

It is also crosslinguistically observed that like logophoric pronouns in African languages, long-distance anaphors generally (albeit perhaps not always) come with point-of-view (or consciousness/awareness) effects. For example, the contrast between (3a) and (3b) below indicates that the referent of the antecedent for Icelandic *sig* "must have an intention to communicate" (Sells 1987a: 451).

(3) Icelandic
    a. Barnið$_1$ lét ekki í ljós að það hefði verið hugsað vel
       the.child put not in light that there had been thought well
       um sig$_1$
       about LDA
       'The child$_1$ didn't reveal that it$_1$ had been taken good care of.'
                                                      (Sells 1987a: 451)
    b. *Barnið$_1$ bar þress ekki merki að það hefði verið hugsað
       the.child bore it not signs that there had been thought
       vel um sig$_1$
       well about LDA
       'The child$_1$ didn't look as if it$_1$ had been taken good care of.'
                                                      (Sells 1987a: 451)

Similarly, the deviance of (4b) is attributed to the fact that John could not have been conscious that he was killed, unlike in the situation of (4a), where John may have been aware that Mary tried to kill him.

(4) Japanese
    a. John$_1$-wa [Mary-ga zibun$_1$-o korosootosita toki] Jane-to
       John-TOP Mary-NOM self-ACC tried.to.kill when Jane-with
       nete ita.
       sleeping was
       'John$_1$ was in bed with Jane when Mary tried to kill him$_1$.'
                                                        (Kuno 1973: 309)

b. *John₁-wa [Mary-ga   zibun₁-o korosita toki] Jane-to
John-TOP Mary-NOM self-ACC killed   when Jane-with
nete   ita.
sleeping was
'John₁ was in bed with Jane when Mary killed him₁.'

(Kuno 1973: 310)

There are other properties that make long-distance anaphors distinct from local anaphors. For example, given appropriate contexts, Japanese *zibun* can refer to the speaker of the utterance instead of being bound by a linguistic antecedent in the sentence. Similarly, Icelandic *sig* can be licensed across sentence boundaries (see, for example, Sells 1987a: 452–453).

All these observations lend empirical support to the claim that certain anaphoric patterns are not governed by structural Binding Conditions. Note, however, that the validity of this claim does not entail that Binding Conditions are unnecessary. Rather, proponents of the third approach generally share the view that a distinction is needed between those anaphoric expressions that are subject to Binding Conditions and those that are constrained by discourse-pragmatic conditions.[2]

Given that there are two distinct mechanisms that pertain to the licensing of anaphoric expressions, one must always make sure which mechanism is involved in the phenomenon under investigation. It must be kept in mind here that just because a given anaphoric expression can be licensed by one mechanism it does not necessarily exclude the possibility that it can be licensed by the other in the same environment. This is a point emphasized by Charnavel and Sportiche (2016). For example, it has been claimed in the literature that English reflexives have an anaphoric and a logophoric use. Picture-noun reflexives are often cited as the quintessential example of the latter use (because they allow split antecedents, can be discourse-bound, etc.) (see Kuno 1987: 125ff.; Pollard and Sag 1992; Reinhart and Reuland 1993, among others). Consider the following sentence.

(5) John showed Bill pictures of themselves.

---

[2] It should be noted that no consensus has been reached among researchers as to whether logophoric binding is a purely discourse-pragmatic phenomenon or it involves a structural mechanism. See Koopman and Sportiche (1989) and Sundaresan (2012).

True, this example shows that the reflexive *themselves* in (5), which takes a split antecedent, behaves like a pronoun rather than a true local anaphor, thereby lending credibility to the claim that a reflexive embedded inside a picture noun phrase is a logophor or, in more neutral terms, an exempt anaphor (so-named because it is exceptionally exempt from standard Binding Conditions). Crucially, however, what this example tells us is that picture-noun reflexives *can* be exempt anaphors, and it does not warrant the conclusion that they *must* be exempt anaphors. This means, then, that we cannot take it for granted that Condition A is irrelevant to the licensing of the reflexive in (6), for instance.

(6)   John likes pictures of himself.

One might be tempted to conclude, based on (5), that *himself* in (6) is not a true anaphor but an exempt anaphor so that it does not fall under Condition A. This is an invalid argument, however, because evidence like (5) does not necessarily rule out the possibility that picture-noun reflexives behave ambiguously—either as exempt anaphors (subject to discourse-pragmatic conditions) or as plain (non-exempt) anaphors (subject to syntactic conditions). What is at issue here is whether the scope of Condition A intersects with the domain in which exempt anaphors are licensed. If they do intersect, sentences like (5) are not informative with respect to the jurisdiction of Condition A. Thus, without taking this possibility into account, one might possibly draw a false descriptive generalization, although, as Charnavel and Sportiche (2016) point out, this has often been overlooked in the literature. (This issue will be discussed in more detail in the next chapter.)

By the same logic, then, we need to be cautious about what we can conclude when we investigate disjoint-reference effects in natural language. The standard Binding Theory posits two disjointness conditions: Conditions B and C. These conditions are structural in the sense that they operate just in case a c-command relation holds between two relevant DPs.[3] Because of its perceived success, the Binding Theory has assumed so

---

[3] Note that even if Condition C and (part of) Condition B are subsumed under Rule I (Grodzinsky and Reinhart 1993; Reinhart 2006; Reinhart 1983), c-command is still relevant because Rule I only applies in a configuration where variable binding is in principle possible.

great an authority that upon encountering disjointness effects in c-command configurations, one might well be tempted to conclude that they must be due to Binding Conditions. However, it has been reported in the literature that natural languages exhibit a phenomenon called antilogophoricity, which gives rise to disjoint-reference effects under certain conditions.[4] To the extent that antilogophoricity and structural Binding Conditions coexist, it is not always a straightforward question whether observed disjoint-reference effects are due to one or the other or both. This means that what have been treated as the consequences of Binding Conditions may turn out to be antilogophoric effects. It should be kept in mind that even if Binding Conditions are actually responsible for the disjointness under investigation, it does not necessarily exclude the possibility that antilogophoricity restrictions may also give rise to the same effect.

The central goal of this book is to bring to light the nature and role of antilogophoricity in the interpretation of anaphora. Unlike logophoric phenomena, which have generated a sizable literature since the mid-1970s, antilogophoric phenomena have scarcely been documented or investigated, and it is not an overstatement to say that the true nature of antilogophoricity is still shrouded in darkness.

That antilogophoricity has not received due attention is by no means accidental; for under normal circumstances the effects of antilogophoricity restrictions tend to be concealed by or masquerade as other independent phenomena, as we will witness in the chapters that follow. It is precisely for this reason that antilogophoric phenomena have gone largely unnoticed for a long time.

The task of elucidating antilogophoricity, however, must not be evaded; in fact, it is of significant relevance to any attempt to formulate an adequate theory of anaphora. This is because, without precisely locating the sources of disjointness, one cannot even describe the conditions governing disjoint-reference phenomena in natural language. If antilogophoricity restrictions and the Binding Theory are independently motivated, it behooves us to, first

---

[4] To my knowledge, the phenomenon of antilogophoricity is discussed at greater or lesser length by Kuno (1986, 1987: 109, 148, 2004), Ruwet (1990), Narahara (1991: 73ff.), Pica (1994), Dubinsky and Hamilton (1998), Liu (2001, 2004), and Patel-Grosz (2012). See also Kuno (1972), Sells (1987b), and Koopman and Sportiche (1989) for observations to the same effect.

and foremost, establish in what ways these two types of conditions operate.

With this aim in mind, this book presents two case studies, —one on overt third-person pronouns in Japanese and one on R-expressions (in particular, names) in English—which I believe will pave the way for a better understanding of the nature and role of antilogophoricity in natural language anaphora. The phenomena featured in these case studies underscore the fact that antilogophoricity may clandestinely play vital roles in determining anaphoric relations.

The remainder of this book is organized as follows. Chapter 2 provides a brief overview of the Binding Theory and (anti)logophoricity, and clarifies the overarching goal of this work. Since the chapter is intended to provide background and set the stage for the discussion in subsequent chapters, I focus mainly on those theoretical concepts and subject matters that are germane to the present study. In particular, I explain why the phenomenon of antilogophoricity needs to be closely investigated. The fundamental issue raised in this chapter concerns not only the present study but any theoretical approach to anaphora.

Chapter 3 submits overt third-person pronouns in Japanese (*kare* 'he' and *kanozyo* 'she') to close scrutiny. It has been known for quite some time that so-called third-person pronouns in Japanese do not pattern with English third-person pronouns in terms of binding-theoretic properties. In particular, Japanese third-person pronouns persistently resist variable binding, although they permit coreference in much the same way as English third-person pronouns do. The prevailing view until quite recently was that overt third-person pronouns in Japanese cannot function as bound variables, and various proposals were put forward to provide a principled account of their alleged unbindability (Montalbetti 1984; Sportiche 1986; Hoji 1990, 1991; Katada 1991; Aoun and Hornstein 1992; Noguchi 1995, 1997; Déchaine and Wiltschko 2002). However, it has been sporadically reported in the literature (Hoji et al. 2000; Hara 2002; see also Hoji 1991, 1997) that there are certain cases in which *kare* and *kanozyo* can be interpreted as bound variables. Chapter 3, therefore, attempts to provide an answer to the question of why Japanese third-person pronouns can be construed as bound variables only in a subset of the contexts in which bound pronouns in English can occur. I argue that the seemingly recalcitrant behavior of Japanese third-person pronouns is due to the fact that antilogophoric effects are at work behind the scenes. Specifically, I claim that overt third-person pronouns in Japanese are, in fact, epithets (i.e., antilogophoric pronouns) so that they can function as bound variables only when Condition B of the Binding Theory and the relevant antilogophoricity constraint are simultaneously satisfied. I further propose that the apparent insensitivity of the referential use of *kare/kanozyo* to the antilogophoricity constraint is attributed to the fact that Japanese, but not English, allows a structure in which a null pronoun is juxtaposed with an appositive epithet phrase.

Chapter 4 discusses the antilogophoric properties of names in English vis-à-vis Condition C of the Binding Theory. It has been widely assumed that names (or more broadly, R-expressions) are subject to Binding Condition C; that is, they must be disjoint in reference from a c-commanding pronoun. For years this condition has been used as a diagnostic test for probing syntactic structures, but the results of this test must be interpreted judiciously. This is because Condition C is not the only disjointness condition that is claimed to apply to names. It has been noted (or hinted) by some researchers (Kuno 1986, 1987, 2004; Sells 1987b; Narahara 1991; Dubinsky and Hamilton 1998; cf. Kuno 1972) that not only epithets but also non-epithetic R-expressions have antilogophoric properties. This means, then, that what one identifies as Condition C effects might be attributed not to Condition C but to antilogophoricity restrictions. This potential confound has often been grossly neglected in the literature but it should not be underestimated given that the two types of disjointness conditions coexist and potentially operate in overlapping environments. It is therefore worthwhile to scrupulously reexamine what have been diagnosed as Condition C violations, and verify whether their putative ungrammaticality actually comes from Condition C. I show that while Condition C and antilogophoric restrictions are independently well-motivated, there is a division of labor between these two constraints in the production of disjoint-reference effects. The findings reported in Chapter 4 point to the necessity of a radical rethinking of the way in which Condition C is computed.

Chapter 5 summarizes the major theoretical and empirical findings of the present study and discusses their theoretical implications.

Chapter 2

Between the Binding Theory and Logophoricity

2.1. Binding Theory

The Binding Theory is concerned with the ways in which referential dependencies are established in natural language. To a first approximation, we may assume that a linguistic expression is bound by another linguistic expression if the value of the former is determined by that of the latter. When it is not bound, it is said to be free. In the following sentence, for instance, the expression *himself* is bound by *John*.

(1) John hates himself.

In (1), the expression *himself* is and must be dependent on *John* for its interpretation, and it cannot have any other value (such as Max, Bill, etc.). In this case, *John*, which determines the value of *himself*, is said to be the *antecedent* of *himself*.

Expressions like *himself*, which we call *anaphors*, are referentially defective in the sense that they must be bound; that is, they must depend on a linguistic antecedent for their interpretation. The defective nature of anaphors is manifested in the fact that they cannot directly refer, which entails, for example, that they cannot be used deictically. Due to this property, an anaphor requires the presence of an appropriate antecedent that binds it, and if there is no such antecedent in the same sentence, the sentence becomes ungrammatical.

(2) (John watched a sad movie.) *Himself cried.

In (2), although it is pragmatically plausible to consider *John* to be the intended antecedent for the anaphor *himself*, the sentence is ungrammatical. This suggests that pragmatic considerations alone are not sufficient to explain how referential dependencies can be established. Similarly, the sentences in (3) are ruled out due to the absence of an appropriate antecedent for the anaphor.

(3) a. *I praise himself.
    b. *People praise himself.
    c. *Mary praises himself.

In English, an anaphor must agree with its antecedent in person, number, and gender.[1] In (3a–c), *I, people,* and *Mary* do not agree with the anaphor *himself* in person, number, and gender, respectively, and hence they do not qualify as an appropriate antecedent for *himself*. Thus, lacking an appropriate binder for the anaphor, these sentences are ruled out as ungrammatical.

Unlike anaphors, (referential) pronouns do not require the presence of a linguistic antecedent in the same sentence, as demonstrated by the following example, where the antecedent for the pronoun is not present in the same sentence.

(4) He cried.

To be more precise, pronouns may or may not be referentially dependent on an antecedent, in a sense to be made clear later. For now it suffices to note that a pronoun may have the same referent as some other noun phrase in the same sentence, as exemplified below.

(5) John$_1$ thinks that he$_1$ will win.

The shared index on *John* and *he* is meant to represent that the two expressions form a referential dependency. Thus, (5) indicates that the sentence is

---

[1] So-called "imposters" constitute a class of exceptions to this. See Collins and Postal (2012).

grammatical with *John* and *he* having an anaphoric relation.

Note that the grammaticality in question is relative to the indexing. For example, (6) represents that the sentence is ungrammatical if *John* and *him* are intended to have the same value. In other words, in (6), *John* and *him* cannot refer to the same person.

(6) *John$_1$ hates him$_1$.

If *him* and *John* are assigned different referential values, the sentence is grammatical, as in (7).[2] (Notice here that the sentence is not starred.)

(7) John$_1$ likes him$_3$.

What is represented here is that the sentence is grammatical if the pronoun *him* does not depend on *John* for its interpretation but rather refers to some male individual whose reference is contextually understood. To be more technical, *him$_3$* represents that the pronoun *him* receives the value that a contextual assignment function assigns to the index 3.[3]

Let us now turn to non-pronominal expressions such as *John*, *the student* and *this man*. Expressions like these, which we call *R-expressions*, are referentially independent. The referential values of R-expressions are determined on the basis of their lexical content and they have fixed reference (in a given context).

Names such as *John* are known as "rigid designators" in the sense that they always pick out the same entity, whereas definite descriptions such as *the teacher* may refer to different individuals depending on the context. It is widely believed that R-expressions must not be bound at all.

We have thus far seen three types of nominal expressions: (i) anaphors, which cannot be interpreted independently, (ii) pronouns, which may or may not be referentially dependent on a linguistic antecedent, and (iii) R-expressions, which are referentially independent.

---

[2] The tacit assumption here is that two noun phrases carrying different indices must refer to different entities, but nothing in our indexing system actually excludes the possibility that the same referential value is assigned to different indices. I defer the discussion of (accidental) coreference until Section 2.4.

[3] An assignment function is a function from the set of natural numbers to individuals.

(8) *Anaphors*
himself, herself, itself, myself, yourself, ourselves, yourselves, themselves, each other, one another

(9) *Pronouns*
he, she, it, I, you, we, him, her, me, us, them, his, her, my, your, our, their

(10) *R-Expressions*
John, that girl, the computer company, the idiot ...

Since the early days of generative grammar, it has been recognized that the ways in which these expressions can be referentially dependent on (or anaphorically related to) other nominal expressions are not determined by context alone but are restricted by certain structural conditions. The standard Binding Theory offers a fairly good approximation of the conditions under which these three types of expressions can/cannot be anaphorically related to antecedents.

(11) *Binding Theory*
   a. *Condition A*
      An anaphor must be bound in its domain.
   b. *Condition B*
      A pronoun must not be bound in its domain.
   c. *Condition C*
      An R-expression must not be bound by a pronoun.

The standard Binding Theory is composed of three conditions: Conditions A, B, and C. While Condition A is a licensing condition for anaphors (reflexives and reciprocals), Conditions B and C can be viewed as anti-licensing conditions that restrict the distributions and interpretations of pronouns and R-expressions, respectively.

There are two technical notions that play central roles here: *c-command* and *local domains*. C-command is a relation between two nodes in a tree that is defined as follows.

(12) *C-Command*
     α c-command β iff α's sister either
     (i) is β, or

(ii) contains β.

Under the classical version of the Binding Theory, binding is defined in terms of c-command and coindexation (i.e., identity of indices).

(13) *Binding*
α binds β iff α c-commands β, and α and β are coindexed.

Strictly speaking, indices as we use them are not the best theoretical device to represent those relations in which one expression is dependent on another. This is because such relations are asymmetric, but indices represent a symmetric relation. The interested reader is referred to Higginbotham (1983) for an alternative notation called *linking*, where headed arrows are used to represent referential dependencies.

It should also be noted that throughout this book, indices are used merely as descriptive devices. Chomsky (1995) states that a "perfect language" should meet the Inclusiveness Condition—a minimalist guideline that permits neither the addition nor removal of non-lexical properties in the course of syntactic computation. The Inclusiveness Condition, therefore, entails that purely theory-internal, non-lexical constructs such as indices should be eschewed since they are not present in the lexicon. Indeed, Chomsky (1995: 228) explicitly states:

(14) [A]ny structure formed by the computation [...] is constituted of elements already present in the lexical items selected for N [= the numeration]; no new objects are added in the course of the computation apart from rearrangement of lexical properties (in particular, **no indices**, bar levels in the sense of X-bar theory, etc. [...]).

[emphasis mine]

Obviously, the question is how indices can be expunged from narrow syntax. One possible approach suggested by Chomsky and Lasnik (1993) is to subsume indexing and interpretive procedures under Binding Conditions themselves. To wit:

(15) *Binding Theory (Chomsky and Lasnik's 1993 version)*
    a. *Condition A*
        If α is an anaphor, interpret it as coreferential with a c-commanding phrase in its domain.

b. *Condition B*
If α is a pronoun, interpret it as disjoint from every c-commanding phrase in its domain.

c. *Condition C*
If α is an R-expression, interpret it as disjoint from every c-commanding phrase.

The Binding Theory thus formulated can enforce Binding Conditions without employing indices (qua syntactic primitives). Chomsky thus proposes that Binding Conditions apply at the conceptual-intentional (C-I) interface.

While I am not committed to the view that indices are genuine syntactic objects, I will use them to indicate intended referential dependencies because they are not only useful for expository purposes but also the most commonly used notation in the generative literature.

Turning now to the notion of local domain, let us assume that the local domain for α is the minimal complete functional complex (CFC) that contains α and in which α's binding condition could, in principle, be satisfied (cf. Chomsky and Lasnik 1993). A CFC is a projection containing all grammatical functions compatible with its head.

With this much in place, let us first take a look at how Condition A accounts for the distribution of anaphors.

(16) *Condition A*
An anaphor must be bound in its local domain.

(17) a. $Fred_1$ likes $himself_1$.
b. *$Fred_1$'s sister likes $himself_1$.
c. *$Fred_1$ thinks that $Maria_2$ likes $himself_1$.
d. *$Fred_1$ likes $Bill_2$'s stories about $himself_1$.
e. $Fred_1$ likes stories about $himself_1$.

In (17a) and (17b), the local domain for the anaphor *himself* is the entire sentence. Sentence (17a) is well-formed because *himself* has a c-commanding antecedent (namely, *Fred*) in its local domain. By contrast, sentence (17b) is ill-formed under the given coindexation because *Fred* does not c-command *himself*, and hence cannot satisfy Condition A, as illustrated below. (For expository purposes, irrelevant details are omitted.)

Chapter 2 Between the Binding Theory and Logophoricity 15

(18)

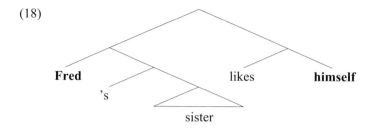

In (17c), the local domain for the anaphor is the embedded clause, as illustrated below.

(19)

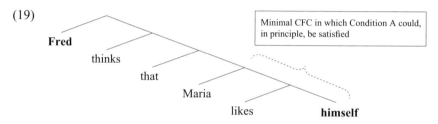

Since the intended antecedent *Fred* is situated outside of the local domain of *himself*, Condition A is not satisfied, hence ungrammaticality. Sentences (17d) and (17e) are quite similar but exhibit different binding possibilities. In (17d), the minimal CFC that contains the anaphor is the DP *Bill's stories about himself*, which contains a potential binder (i.e., *Bill*) for the anaphor. Thanks to the presence of a potential binder, this CFC is one in which the binding condition for an anaphor could, in principle, be satisfied, and hence counts as the local domain where Condition A applies, as illustrated below.

(20)

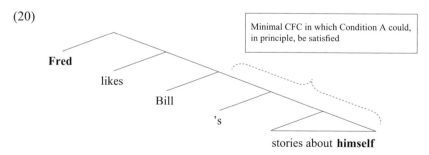

Here, *Fred* lies outside of the local domain of the anaphor *himself*, and it thus cannot be taken as antecedent of *himself*. In (17e), by contrast, there

16   *Antilogophoricity and Binding Theory*

is no potential binder for the anaphor within the DP *stories about himself*, and hence this DP does not count as the local domain for *himself* (precisely because Condition A could not even in principle be satisfied). The local domain is, therefore, the entire sentence, as shown below.

(21)

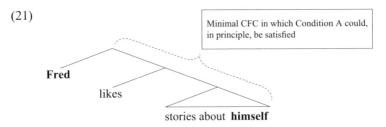

Hence, *Fred* can bind *himself*, satisfying Condition A.

Let us now consider Condition B.

(22) *Condition B*
A pronoun must not be bound in its local domain.

(23) a. *Fred₁ likes him₁.
b. Fred₁'s sister likes him₁.
c. Fred₁ thinks that Maria₂ likes him₁.
d. Fred₁ likes Bill₂'s stories about him₁.
e. Fred₁ likes stories about him₁.

In (23a) and (23b), the local domain for the pronoun *him* is the entire sentence. Condition B is violated in (23a) because the pronoun *him* is bound by *Fred* in its domain. In (23b), the pronoun is free in its domain because it is not c-commanded by the antecedent *Fred*. Condition B is thus satisfied. In (23c), the local domain for the pronoun is the embedded clause, as illustrated below.

(24)

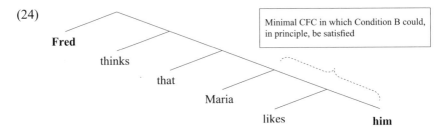

Chapter 2 Between the Binding Theory and Logophoricity

The pronoun *him* is free in its local domain (i.e., the embedded clause), and hence Condition B is satisfied. The examples in (23d) and (23e) show that the local domain for a pronoun is computed in a slightly different way than that for an anaphor. Recall that pronouns do not need a binder. Then the presence or absence of a potential binder does not affect the size of the local domain for a pronoun.

Thus, in (23d), the local domain for *him* is *Bill's stories about him*.

(25)

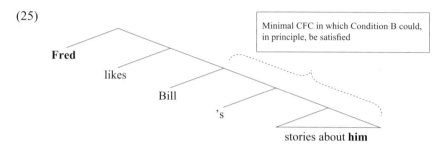

Likewise, in (23e), the local domain for *him* is *stories about him*.

(26)

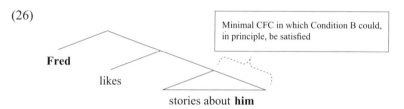

Since the pronoun is free in its local domain in both (23d) and (23e), *Fred* can be taken as antecedent of *him* in both cases.

Finally, let us consider Condition C. Condition C is defined as follows.[4]

(27) *Condition C*
 An R-expression must not be bound by a pronoun.

(28) a. *He$_1$ likes Fred$_1$.
 b. *He$_1$ thinks that Maria$_2$ likes Fred$_1$.
 c. His$_1$ mother likes Fred$_1$.
 d. [Those who know him$_1$] like Fred$_1$.

---

[4] While there are several extant versions of Condition C, this one is commonly accepted as descriptively adequate.

18   *Antilogophoricity and Binding Theory*

The sentences in (28a)–(28b) demonstrate that *Fred*, an R-expression, cannot take a c-commanding pronoun—whether local or remote—as its antecedent. Condition C, as formulated in (27), amounts to saying that an R-expression cannot be anaphorically related to any c-commanding pronoun. This is schematically represented in the following diagram.

(29) *Pronoun = R-expression

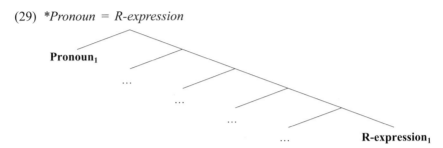

Note that the ill-formedness of (28a) and (28b) has nothing to do with the linear order between the R-expression and the pronoun that corefers with it. This is demonstrated by the well-formedness of (28c) and (28d), where the pronoun is followed by a name that it corefers with, just as in (28a) and (28b).

2.2. Challenges to the Binding Theory

We have looked at how the standard Binding Theory captures the distribution and interpretation of nominal expressions (anaphors, pronouns, and R-expressions). At least at the descriptive level, the standard Binding Theory appears to be a successful attempt that nicely accounts for the interpretive dependencies between nominal expressions. However, ever since the advent of Chomsky's (1981, 1986) Binding Theory, a myriad of empirical challenges within English and across languages have been reported, suggesting that anaphoric patterns in natural languages may well be constrained in more complex and nuanced ways.

For example, it has been reported that certain types of anaphors may be discourse-bound, contradicting the fundamental assumption that an anaphor is grammatically required to have a local antecedent. As shown below, picture-noun reflexives are allowed to have a discourse antecedent under appropriate contexts.

(30) a. John₁ was furious. The picture of himself₁ in the museum had been mutilated.
b. Mary₁ was extremely upset. That picture of herself₁ on the front page of the *Times* would circulate all over the world.

(Pollard and Sag 1992: 268)

Despite the fact that *himself* in (30a) and *herself* in (30b) do not have an antecedent within the same sentence, both examples are acceptable.

Another challenge to the standard Binding Theory comes from the fact that in certain cases, anaphors may take a non-c-commanding antecedent.

(31) The fact that there is a picture of himself₁ hanging in the post office is believed (by Mary) to be disturbing Tom₁.

(Jackendoff 1972: 137)

(32) The agreement that [Iran and Iraq]₁ reached guaranteed each other₁'s trading rights in the disputed waters until the year 2010.

(Pollard and Sag 1992: 264)

In (31) and (32), the reflexive *himself* and the reciprocal *each other* are anteceded by a non-c-commanding DP, contrary to the prediction of the standard Binding Theory.

Furthermore, there are cases in which anaphors can take a split antecedent (Lebeaux 1984: 345–346, among others).

(33) John told Mary that there were some pictures of themselves inside.

(Lebeaux 1984: 346)

The facts shown in (30)–(33) are not immediately amenable to the standard Binding Theory. Upon closer scrutiny, however, it is not the case that just any kind of anaphor can behave this way.

(34) (Mary₁ was furious.) *The article criticized herself₁.

(35) *The fact that Sue likes himself₁ is believed (by Mary) to be disturbing Tom₁.

(Pollard and Sag 1992: 265)

(36) %John showed Mary themselves (in the mirror).

When an anaphor is a direct argument of a verb, as in (34)–(36), discourse binding, non-c-commanding binding, and split antecedence are consistently disallowed.

These observations suggest that it is necessary to distinguish between anaphors that are regulated by a grammatical condition and anaphors that are exempt from it. The question that immediately arises is: On what basis are these two types to be separated?

A widely held view is that a plain (i.e., non-exempt) anaphor is one whose antecedent is a coargument of the same predicate (Pollard and Sag 1992; Reinhart and Reuland 1993, among others; cf. Safir 2004a). The idea, roughly, is that an anaphor must be bound by a syntactic coargument antecedent if there is one, and it is exempt otherwise.

Recall at this point that under the standard Binding Theory, the domain of Condition A is assumed to be flexible such that in the absence of a potential binder, an anaphor extends its binding domain to seek one. Thus, the coargument-based theory and the standard Binding Theory have different slants on the anaphoric pattern exemplified below.

(37) Bill remembered that Tom_1 saw [a picture of $himself_1$] in the post office.

(Pollard and Sag 1992: 271)

In this case, the given coindexing is obligatory. Condition A of the standard Binding Theory correctly predicts that *himself* must be bound by *Tom* (and not *Bill*) because the minimal CFC that has a potential binder for the anaphor is the embedded clause.

Under the coargument-based theory, by contrast, the reflexive here must be exempt, as it has no coargument antecedent. Hence the fact that *himself* cannot take *Bill* as its antecedent must be explained not in terms of grammatical constraints but in some other way.

It is worth noting at this point that exempt anaphors are widely viewed as closely related to logophoricity. The reason is that they exhibit characteristic properties of logophoric pronouns. For example, it has been reported that the antecedent of an exempt anaphor must refer to the individual whose perspective (or point of view) is presented in the context. The following contrast illustrates this.

(38) John₁ was going to get even with Mary. That picture of himself₁ in the paper would really annoy her, as would the other stunts he had planned.

(Pollard and Sag 1992: 274)

(39) *Mary was quite taken aback by the publicity John₁ was receiving. That picture of himself₁ in the paper had really annoyed her, and there was not much she could do about it.

(Pollard and Sag 1992: 274)

The sentences in (38) are narrated from John's perspective; in other words, John is an internal protagonist in this context. This contrasts with (39), where Mary is presented as an internal protagonist (or a perspective holder). In the former case, *John* can be taken as antecedent of the picture-noun reflexive *himself*, while in the latter case, the picture-noun reflexive cannot be anaphoric to *John*, suggesting that exempt anaphors must refer to the individual from whose perspective the relevant report is made.

Another characteristic of exempt anaphors is that they show intervention effects in much the same way as the Super Equi phenomenon, a phenomenon wherein PRO is controlled by an argument of a predicate sitting in a superordinate clause (Grinder 1970). For example, in the following sentence, PRO is controlled by a remote antecedent.

(40) Roxanne₁ knew that it would be difficult PRO₁ to criticize herself/*himself.

Of particular relevance to our discussion is that Super Equi is blocked in the presence of a potential controller (Grinder 1970; Clements 1974, among others).

(41) *Eric₁ said that Roxanne knew that it would be difficult PRO₁ to criticize himself.

(adapted from Grinder 1970: 303)

(42) Eric said that Roxanne₁ knew that it would be difficult PRO₁ to criticize herself₁.

(adapted from Grinder 1970: 303)

Note that inanimate or expletive subjects do not prevent Super Equi because they do not qualify as potential controllers.

(43) John thought [that Proposition 91 made [PRO undressing himself] illegal].

(Pollard and Sag 1992: 273)

(44) John thought [that it was likely to be illegal [PRO to undress himself]].

(Pollard and Sag 1992: 273)

Returning to the sentence in (37), repeated below as (45), the fact that *Bill* cannot antecede the picture noun reflexive is seen as an intervention effect under the coargument-based theory.

(45) Bill₁ remembered that Tom₂ saw [a picture of himself*₁/₂] in the post office.

That is, it is the presence of the potential intervening antecedent *Tom* that makes it impossible for *himself* to be anteceded by *Bill*. Evidence in support of this account comes from the fact that replacing *Tom* with an inanimate (or expletive) DP makes it possible for the picture-noun reflexive to be anaphoric to *Bill*.

(46) ?Bill₁ remembered that the Times had printed [a picture of himself₁] in the Sunday edition.

(Pollard and Sag 1992: 272)

These facts indicate that picture-noun reflexives (or more generally, reflexives in non-coargument domains) can behave as exempt anaphors, unlike reflexives in coargument position.

One might therefore be tempted to conclude that the standard Binding Theory should be jettisoned in favor of the coargument-based theory. While it is plausible to assume that a distinction exists between plain and exempt anaphors, the data we have observed above do not necessarily undermine the standard Binding Theory. We have seen, for example, various examples where picture-noun reflexives are exempt from Condition A, but the conclusion we can draw from them is that they *can* be exempt anaphors, and not that they *must* be. There is no a priori reason to reject the possibility that the domain in which exempt anaphors are licensed intersects with the domain in which non-exempt anaphors are licensed by Condition A. This means that we cannot assume gratuitously that Condition A is irrelevant to the licensing of the reflexive in (47), for example.

(47) Tom$_1$ saw [a picture of himself$_1$].

It is often assumed (explicitly or implicitly) that the two types of anaphors can be distinguished in terms of coargumenthood, but Charnavel and Sportiche (2016) point out that previous studies reached this conclusion without taking into account the possibility that anaphors may behave ambiguously either as plain or as exempt anaphors. They caution that it is only when this potential confounding factor is controlled for that we can precisely delineate the domain of Condition A.

Charnavel and Sportiche employed French anaphors *son propre* "his/its own" and *elle-même* "herself/itself" to shed light on the scope of Condition A. Capitalizing on the fact that *son propre* and *elle-même* can take inanimate antecedents, they closely investigated the anaphoric patterns these anaphors display with inanimate antecedents. The idea is that if the antecedent of an anaphor is inanimate, it is guaranteed that that anaphor must be plain (and cannot be exempt) because inanimate entities do not qualify as a perspective/point-of-view holder (or the center of consciousness, an empathic target, etc.). Their investigation of inanimate (therefore unambiguously plain) anaphors revealed, contrary to the assumption of the coargument-based theory, that the domain of Condition A is, in fact, essentially identical to what is assumed under the standard Binding Theory.

It is by now widely acknowledged that the structural binding condition licensing a plain anaphor should be distinguished from the conditions whereby logophors are licensed, but the lesson that Charnavel and Sportiche's findings teach us is that these two types of conditions may conspire to obscure the true nature of the phenomenon under investigation. Most importantly, they show that just because an anaphor can be licensed by one mechanism in a given environment, it does not necessarily follow that it cannot be licensed in some other way in the same environment.

By the same logic, then, just because a given anaphoric dependency is disallowed by one mechanism in a given environment, there is no reason to exclude the possibility that it can be blocked by some other mechanism in the same context. This is the very reason that antilogophoricity must be closely investigated.

If antilogophoricity and Binding Conditions (B and C) are two independent disjointness requirements, the question arises as to whether observed disjoint-reference effects are due to one or the other or both (or possibly neither). Then, without knowing what exactly antilogophoricity restrictions cover, one might mistakenly diagnose antilogophoric effects as the consequences of Binding Conditions. Note that even if Binding Conditions are actually relevant to the disjoint-reference effect under investigation, it does not necessarily exclude the possibility that antilogophoricity restrictions may also bring about the same effect. Therefore, to fully understand the mechanisms of disjoint-reference phenomena in natural language, it is important to study the nature and role of antilogophoricity, and without undertaking this task, one cannot even provide adequate descriptions of disjointness conditions.

2.3. Logophoricity

Since our investigation capitalizes on insights from the wealth of research on logophoricity, it is worthwhile to take a close look at the basic properties of logophoricity before we embark on the journey of antilogophoricity.

The term "logophoric pronoun" (*pronom logophorique*) was coined by Hagège (1974) and has been widely used since. Clements (1975: 141) states that logophoric pronouns are used "to distinguish reference to the individual whose speech, thoughts, or feelings are reported or reflected in a given context, from reference to other individuals". Logophoricity is characterized mainly along two dimensions: (i) logophoric domains, by which I mean those contexts in which logophors can occur, and (ii) logocentric antecedents, i.e., possible antecedents for logophoric pronouns.

According to Clements, the following characteristics are typically observed for logophoric pronouns across languages:

(48) a. logophoric pronouns are restricted to *reportive contexts* transmitting the words or thoughts of an individual or individuals other than the speaker or narrator;
 b. the antecedent does not occur in the same reportive context as the logophoric pronoun;

c. the antecedent designates the individual or individuals whose words or thoughts are transmitted in the reported context in which the logophoric pronoun occurs.

(Clements 1975: 171-172)

Clements himself admits that it is hard to define "reportive contexts" in a way relevant to logophoricity. This becomes even more evident when we look at crosslinguistic variation in logophoric domains.

2.3.1. Logophoric Domains

2.3.1.1. Logophoric Domain 1: Complement Clauses of Verbs of Speech

Since the primary function of logophors is to indicate coreference with the source of reported speech, logophors across languages can occur in complement clauses of verbs of saying, whether they are realized as logophoric pronouns, affixes, clitics, or long-distance reflexives.

(49) Mundang
  à   rí   ʒì   Iwà fàn   sā:
  Pro say LOG find thing beauty
  'He$_1$ said that he$_1$ had found something beautiful.'

(Hagège 1974: 291)

(50) Gokana
  aè kɔ   aè dɔ-ɛ̀
  he said he fell-LOG
  'He$_1$ said that he$_1$ fell.'

(Hyman and Comrie 1981: 20)

(51) Ewe
  Kofi be yè-dzo
  Kofi say LOG-leave
  'Kofi$_1$ said that he$_1$ left.'

(Clements 1975: 142)

(52) Japanese
Taroo-wa zibun-ga sono hon-o mituketa to itta.
Taro-TOP self-NOM that book-ACC found COMP said
'Taro₁ said that he₁ had found that book.'

2.3.1.2. Logophoric Domain 2: Complements of Verbs of Thought, Psychological State and Perception

In many languages, logophoric forms can be found not only in complement clauses of verbs of saying but also in clauses embedded under other classes of verbs such as verbs of thought or cognition. Stirling (1993: 259) suggests that there is an implicational universal hierarchy (shown below) according to which languages restrict the set of domains in which logophoric forms can be employed.

(53) *Logocentric Verb Hierarchy*
communication > thought > psychological state > perception

Likewise, Culy (2002: 202), building on Culy (1994), proposes the following implicational hierarchy.

(54) speech > thought > non-factive perception > knowledge > direct perception

The idea is that if verbs in one category can introduce logophoric contexts, then so too can verbs in all the higher categories.

The psych verb construction is another well-attested logophoric domain. In examples (55)–(58), the antecedent of the logophoric pronoun is the experiencer, whose mental state is being reported.

(55) Ewe
dyi dzɔ Ama be yè-dyi vi
heart straighten Ama that LOG-bear child
'Ama₁ was happy that she₁ bore a child.'
(Clements 1975: 162)

(56) Gokana
pɔ̀ síí   lébàrè kɔ aè dɔ-ɛ̀
fear catches Lebare that he fell-LOG
'Lebare₁ is afraid that he₁ fell.'

(Hyman and Comrie 1981: 21)

(57) Eleme
è-wāā   kɔ̀   ɛ̀-dɔ̀-ɛ̀
he-be.angry that 3-fall-LOG
'He₁ was angry that he₁ fell.'

(Bond 2006: 239)

(58) Japanese
Zibun-ga   baka-na   koto-ga   Taroo-o   kanasimaseta.
self-NOM   fool-COP COMP-NOM   Taro-ACC   saddened
'That he₁ was a fool saddened Taro₁.'

(Kuno 1978: 194)

Direct perception predicates are at the lowest in the implicational hierarchy proposed by Culy (1994, 2002), but this does not mean that no languages allow them to introduce a logophoric domain. In Boko, for instance, the complement clause of a direct perception verb constitutes a logophoric domain.

(59) Boko
ā   'è   álɛ́   lélɛ̀
3SG.PFAT see.PERF 3SG.PROG.LOG fall.PROG
'He saw himself falling.'

(Jones 1998: 155)

2.3.1.3. Logophoric Domain 3: Adverbial Clauses

The distribution of logophors extends far beyond the context of what is normally conceived of as reported speech. It is not always the case that logophoric domains are introduced by particular embedding verbs; some languages allow adverbial clauses, relative clauses, and simple (non-embedded) clauses to form logophoric domains.

For example, it is not crosslinguistically uncommon for purpose clauses to form logophoric domains.

(60) Ewe
Kofi wɔ-wɔ-m be Kɔku va yè gbɔ
Kofi RED-do that Koku come LOG side
'Kofi₁ is arranging for Koku to come to him₁.'

(Clements 1975: 155)

(61) Gokana
lébàreè dù kɔ baá mɔn-ɛ̀ɛ̀ ɛ
Lebare came that they see-LOG him
'Lebare₁ came for them to see him₁.'

(Hyman and Comrie 1981: 30)

(62) Babungo
ŋwɔ́ nyiŋ láā kɨ́ vɔ̌ŋ sáŋ yí mē
he ran that NEG they beat LOG not
'He₁ ran away so that they could not beat him₁.'

(Schaub 1985: 111)

In (60), the event of Koku's coming has not taken place, so that it is "not yet a matter of objective fact, but remains in the sphere of Kofi's intention" (Clements 1975: 155–156), which, according to Clements, makes it possible for the external speaker to take on the viewpoint of Kofi to report the event. The following minimal pair (taken from Clements 1975: 160–161) further shows that purpose clauses can serve as a domain that is associated with the point of view of an internal protagonist.

(63) Ewe
dɛvi-a xɔ tohehe be yè-agada alakpa ake o
child-DEF receive punishment so that LOG-tell lie again NEG
'The child₁ received punishment so that he₁ wouldn't tell lies again.'

(64) Ewe
dɛvi-a xɔ tohehe be wò-agada alakpa ake o
child-DEF receive punishment so that Pro-tell lie again NEG
'The child₁ received punishment so that he₁/₂ wouldn't tell lies again.'

The two sentences in (63) and (64) above are identical except that the former involves a logophoric pronoun, whereas the latter an ordinary third-person pronoun. In both cases, the embedded pronoun can be interpreted as coreferential with the matrix subject, but there is a subtle difference in meaning. The sentence in (63) is interpreted as conveying that the child voluntarily received punishment (for his own purpose of preventing himself from lying), while the sentence in (64) is most naturally interpreted as expressing that the child received punishment against his will (and someone else has an intention of stopping his habit of lying) (Clements 1975: 161). Thus, Clements notes that some speakers find (63) anomalous on the grounds that such a situation is unlikely to happen.

The same observation can be made for the Japanese reflexive *zibun* when it is used in a purpose clause. That is, the occurrence of *zibun* in such a context implies that the purpose in question is being narrated from the perspective of the internal speaker rather than that of the external speaker. In (65) below, for example, the child is understood to have voluntarily received punishment for his own sake of not telling lies again (and thus the situation described by the sentence is somewhat unlikely to occur).

(65) Japanese
Sono ko-wa [nidoto zibun-ga uso-o tuk-anai yooni]
that child-TOP ever.again self-NOM lie-ACC tell-NEG AUX
batu-o uketa.
punishment-ACC received
'The child received punishment in order not to tell lies again.'

If *zibun* in (65) is replaced with a null pronoun, it does not necessarily mean that the child voluntarily received punishment.

(66) Japanese
Sono ko-wa [nidoto uso-o tuk-anai yooni]
that child-TOP ever.again lie-ACC tell-NEG AUX
batu-o uketa.
punishment-ACC received
'The child received punishment in order not to tell lies again.'

In certain languages, logophoric domains extend even further to other types of adverbial clauses. Some examples are given below.

(67) Gokana
lébàreè dìv im bòò beè kɔɔ́ mm̀ de-è   a   gíã́
Lebare hit me because that I   ate-LOG his yams
'Lebare₁ hit me because I ate his₁ yams.'
(Hyman and Comrie 1981: 30)

(68) Boko
a. aalɛ́   kɛ lá wā   ye   kúlá-ɔ   gbaɛ́ wà
   3Pl.PROG act as 3Pl.STAT.LOG want anchor-Pl release like
   'They₁ were acting as if they₁ wanted to release anchors.'
(Jones 1998: 158)

b. Bíɔ zɔ́á dɔ̀   Sàbí wà kɛ́   à   'í
   Bio noise emit.PERF Sabi DAT because 3SG.PERF water
   kɔ̀lɛ   wa   yã́í
   spill.PERF.3SG 3SG.DAT.LOG reason
   'Bio₁ rebuked Sabi because he spilt water on him₁.'
(Jones 1998: 158)

c. à   zɔ́lɛ   'e   à   mɔ̀
   3SG.PERF sit.PERF until 3SG.PERF come.PERF
   a   kíí
   3SG.POSS.LOG place
   'He₁ sat down until he came to him₁.'
(Jones 2000: 148)

(69) Japanese
a. John-wa [Mary-ga   zibun-o hihansite   iru toki] tonari
   John-TOP Mary-NOM   self-ACC criticizing is when next
   no   heya-ni   ita.
   GEN room-LOC was
   'John₁ was in the next room when Mary was criticizing him₁.'
(Kuno 1973: 312)

b. Takasi-wa [Yosiko-ga   mizu-o   zibun-no ue-ni
   Takasi-TOP Yoshiko-NOM   water-ACC self-GEN on-LOC
   kobosita node]   nuretesimatta.
   spilled because got.wet
   'Takashi₁ got wet because Yoshiko spilled water on him₁.'
(Sells 1987a: 455)

c. Taroo-wa [Hanako-ga   zibun-o   hihansita noni] nanimo
    Taro-TOP   Hanako-NOM self-ACC   criticized though anything
    iw-anakat-ta.
    say-NEG-PAST
    'Taro₁ said nothing though Hanako criticized him₁.'

(Iida 1996: 62)

In each of these cases, the logophoric form is licensed even though the embedded clause does not seem, in any obvious sense, to be reporting on the speech, thoughts or perceptions of the referent of the logocentric antecedent.

2.3.1.4. Logophoric Domain 4: Relative Clauses

In some languages, relative clauses constitute a logophoric domain but there are some complications with the licensing of logophoric forms in this construction.

In Ewe, relative clauses themselves do not serve as logophoric domains, as evidenced by the fact that the logophoric pronoun *yè* is not licensed.

(70) Ewe
      *Ama   ɖo   ŋku nyɔnuvi hi   dze yè   gbɔ dyi
      Ama   set eye girl   REL stay LOG side on
      'Ama₁ remembered the girl who stayed with her₁.'

(Clements 1975: 156)

However, the otherwise disallowed occurrence of a logophoric pronoun in a relative clause is permitted if the sentence containing the relative clause is embedded under a predicate that is capable of introducing a logophoric domain.

(71) Ewe
      Ama₁ gblɔ be yè-ɖo   ŋku nyɔnuvi hi   dze yè₁ gbɔ dyi
      Ama say that LOG-set eye girl   REL stay LOG side on
      'Ama₁ said that she₁ remembered the girl who stayed with her₁.'

(Clements 1975: 156)

A similar observation can be made for Mundani, where a relative clause is not in itself a logophoric domain. In this language, a logophoric pronoun can be used in a relative clause if the relative clause occurs with a particular nominal (such as *àghī* 'thing') that expresses the content of what is said, thought or felt.

(72) Mundani
tà kő àghī yū yé ā lɔ́'ɔ́ ghǐ lá
he know thing that LOG IMPF F1 do SBRD
'He₁ knows what he₁ will do.'

(Parker 1986: 155)

The "domino effect" (i.e., a phenomenon wherein non-logophoric domains are rendered transparent to logophor licensing when contained within a superordinate logophoric domain) is a fairly robust phenomenon but is not universal. For example, Mundang disallows the use of a logophoric pronoun in a relative clause even if a logocentric predicate is present in the preceding clause (Hagège 1974: 294; Stirling 1993: 262). In other words, relative clauses in this language are completely opaque to logophoric effects.

Still other languages allow logophoric pronouns to appear in relative clauses rather freely, irrespective of the type of the predicate in a higher clause. One such language is Tuburi (Hagège 1974). In this language, the complementizer *gā* has incorporated into the relative clause marker *ma:gā*, by virtue of which logophoric pronouns can be systematically licensed in relative clauses. Note, however, that in Boko, where the complementizer and the relative pronoun are unrelated, logophoric pronouns nevertheless can readily occur in relative clauses (Jones 1998, 2000).

(73) Boko
a. à 'íkō kpà kíá pɔ́ á
3SG.PERF authority give.PERF king REL 3SG.PFAT.LOG
kpà wà
give.PERF DAT
'He₁ gave authority to the king that he₁ installed.'

(Jones 1998: 157)

b. à   wɛ́ pà̰   gbɛ̃́   pɔ́   liaa
    3SG.PERF eye cross.PERF person REL surround
    a   zi-ɔ   la
    3SG.O.LOG ADES-Pl over
    'He₁ cast his eye over those who were around him₁.'

(Jones 1998: 157)

c. Lùa ì   kpá   gbɛ̃́   pɔ́   lɛ́   a
    God 3SG.HAB give person REL PROG 3SG.POSS.LOG
    yá̰   ma-ɔ   wà
    word hear-Pl DAT
    'God₁ gives it to those who obey his₁ word.'

(Jones 1998: 164)

Likewise, Japanese, which lacks overt relative pronouns, is quite liberal in the use of *zibun* within relative clauses (though there are some constraints, as we will see in Chapter 4).

(74) Japanese
    a. Taroo-wa [RC zibun-ga   katta]   hon-o   yonda.
        Taro-TOP   self-NOM bought   magazine-ACC read
        'Taro₁ read the book that he₁ had bought.'
    b. Taroo-wa [RC zibun-o   hihansiteiru] kizi-o   yonda.
        Taro-TOP   self-ACC criticize   article-ACC read
        'Taro₁ read the article that criticized him₁.'

2.3.1.5. Logophoric Domain 5: Simple Clauses

In some languages, logophoric forms can occur not only in subordinate clauses but also in simple clauses, as exemplified below.

(75) Boko
    à   bā   fìa   a   zi
    he.PERF rope wind.PERF 3SG.O.LOG ADES
    'He₁ wound a rope around him₁.'

(Jones 1998: 159)

It is also worth noting that logophoric pronouns are often found in the possessor position of a possessive noun phrase. Jones (2000: 147) points out that this has often been overlooked in the literature presumably because it does not fit the classic definition of logophoricity.

Ngiti is among those languages that have a set of logophoric possessive pronouns. As the following contrast demonstrates, the use of a non-logophoric possessive pronoun instead of a logophoric possessive indicates that the possessor is disjoint in reference from the subject.

(76) Ngiti
    a. k-ù'à   kà-pfɔ̃
        3SG-cut.PERF.PRES 3SG-foot
        'He$_1$ has cut his$_2$ foot.'
                                                  (Kutsch Lojenga 1994: 212)
    b. k-ù'à   pfɔ̃-na
        3SG-cut.PERF.PRES foot-3SG.LOG.POSS
        'He$_1$ has cut his$_1$ (own) foot.'
                                                  (Kutsch Lojenga 1994: 212)

Logophoric possessive pronouns should not simply be viewed as a means to indicate coreference between the possessor and the subject. The Boko examples in (77) demonstrate that there are cases in which non-subjects can antecede logophoric possessive pronouns.[5]

(77) Boko
    a. à   nɛ́   kù   a   'ɔ   wà
        3SG.PERF child catch.PERF 3SG.POSS.LOG hand DAT
        'He$_1$ caught the child$_2$ by his$_2$ hand.'
                                                                (Jones 1998: 163)
    b. à   yǎ   'ò-ɛ̀   a
        1SG.PERF word speak.PERF-3SG.BEN 3SG.POSS.LOG
        kpɛ́-ú
        house-in
        'I spoke to him$_1$ in his$_1$ house.'
                                                                 (Jones 1998: 163)

In Ngiti and Japanese, a logophoric pronoun and its antecedent can be coar-

---

[5] If there is more than one potential antecedent for a logophoric possessive pronoun, the logophoric pronoun is interpreted as coreferential with the subject. I assume that this is due to an independent constraint disfavoring ambiguity.

guments of the same predicate.

(78) Ngiti
k`-àla   ndɨ
3SG-see:PERF.PRES 3SG.LOG
'He has seen himself.'

(Kutsch Lojenga 1994: 211)

(79) Japanese
Taroo-wa zibun-o mita.
Taro-TOP self-ACC saw
'Taro saw himself.'

In regard to Japanese *zibun*, there is a view that locally bound *zibun*, though homophonous with its long-distance counterpart, is governed by structural binding (Sells 1987a: 450, fn. 6; Abe 1997; cf. Oshima 2004, 2007; Kishida 2011 for a three-way classification of *zibun*). I will come back to this point in Chapter 4, where *zibun* is used as a diagnostic tool for identifying potential logocentric antecedents.

2.3.2. Logocentric Antecedents

We have seen a variety of contexts where logophoric forms are licensed. Although languages display a diverse array of patterns in logophoric domains, it seems that variation is restricted to a limited range of options, and there are certain implicational universals with respect to the way languages circumscribe the range of possible logophoric domains (see Hyman and Comrie (1981), Stirling (1993), Culy (1994, 2002), Huang (2000) for further details).

To understand logophoric phenomena, it is also important to consider what qualifies as a possible antecedent for a logophor.

There is a marked tendency for logocentric antecedents to be grammatical subjects. However, it should be emphasized that despite the fact that subject orientation is quite pervasive across languages, being a grammatical subject is neither a necessary nor a sufficient condition for qualifying as a logocentric antecedent, as stressed by Clements (1975) and many others. In the following Ewe sentence, for instance, either *Ama* or *Kofi* can be an antecedent for the logophoric pronoun *yè*, suggesting that it is not subjecthood that determines the possible antecedents for the logophor.

(80) Ewe
Ama se tso Kofi gbɔ be yè-xɔ nunana
Ama hear from Kofi side that LOG-receive gift
'Ama$_1$ heard from Kofi$_2$ that she$_1$/he$_2$ received a gift.'

(Clements 1975: 159)

Here, what makes it possible for *Kofi* to antecede the logophor is the fact that Kofi is the source of the report.

Likewise, it is widely assumed that the Japanese reflexive *zibun* must be anteceded by a structural subject (Inoue 1976; Shibatani 1978; Katada 1991, among many others), but it is not difficult to find cases in which non-subjects can be taken as antecedents for *zibun*.

(81) Sono keiken-wa Mary$_1$-ni zibun$_1$-ga baka dearu
that experience-TOP Mary-to self-NOM fool is
koto-o osieta.
COMP-ACC taught
'That experience taught Mary$_1$ that she$_1$ was a fool.'

(Kuno 1972: 190)

(82) John-no zisatu-wa Mary$_1$-nitotte zibun$_1$-ga kare-ni
John-GEN suicide-TOP Mary-to self-NOM he-by
uragir-are-ta koto-o imisita.
betray-PASS-PAST COMP-ACC meant
'John's suicide meant to Mary$_1$ that she$_1$ had been betrayed by him.'

(Kuno 1972: 190)

(83) Ken$_1$-wa Naomi$_2$-o zibun$_{1/2}$-no uti-e kaesi-ta.
Ken-TOP Naomi-ACC self-GEN house-to return-PAST
'Ken$_1$ sent Naomi$_2$ back to his$_1$/her$_2$ house.'

(Kitagawa 1981: 62)[6]

---

[6] Kitagawa (1981) reports that the sentence is ungrammatical if the subject *Ken* is taken as antecedent of *zibun*, but for many speakers it is just as grammatical as when the object *Naomi* is intended to be the antecedent of *zibun*.

(84) Taroo₁-wa Hanako₂-kara zibun₁/₂-ga katta toiu hookoku-o
Taro-TOP Hanako-from self-NOM won COMP report-ACC
uketa.
got
'Taro₁ got a report from Hanako₂ that he₁/she₂ won.'

(Iida 1996: 71)

(85) Taroo₁-wa Hanako₂-ni zibun₁/₂-no ten-o osiete-yat-ta.
Taro-TOP Hanako-DAT self-GEN score-ACC tell-give-PAST
'Taro₁ told Hanako₂ his₁/her₂ scores.'

(Iida 1996: 73)

Given that subjecthood is not crucial, what exactly determines the antecedent of a logophor? Sells (1987a) offers a taxonomy of discourse roles that is useful in characterizing logocentric antecedents.

(86) a. SOURCE: The one who makes the report; the intentional agent of the communication
b. SELF: The one whose mental state or attitude the content of the proposition describes
c. PIVOT: The one from whose point of view the report is made; the one with respect to whose (space-time) location the content of the proposition is evaluated

In Sells's theory, each of these discourse roles is assigned to either the "external" speaker (i.e., the current speaker of the utterance) or some "internal" protagonist in the discourse. Sells claims that logophoric phenomena are classified into three types (listed below), depending on the assignment of these three roles.

	"Logophoric" verb	*Psych-verb*	*3POV*
SOURCE	internal	external	external
SELF	internal	internal	external
PIVOT	internal	internal	internal

Table 2.1 Types of Logophoricity

In the logophoric-verb (or "fully logophoric") environment, all three roles are linked to an internal protagonist. This is instantiated by indirect discourse contexts, as in (87) below.

(87) Japanese
Taroo$_1$-wa [Yosiko-ga zibun$_1$-o aisiteiru to] itta.
Taro-TOP Yoshiko-NOM self-ACC love COMP said
'Taro$_1$ said that Yoshiko loved him$_1$.'

(Sells 1987a: 461)

In (87), *Taroo*, being the subject of the verb *say*, is understood as the SOURCE (as well as the SELF and the PIVOT) with respect to the embedded proposition.

In the psych-verb environment, where the external speaker reports the mental state or attitude of an internal referent, the speaker of the utterance carries the SOURCE role, while the other two roles are associated with the internal protagonist. An example is given below.

(88) Japanese
[Yosiko-ga zibun$_1$-o musisita koto]-ga Taroo$_1$-o
 Yoshiko-NOM self-ACC ignored COMP-NOM Taro-ACC
yuuutunisita.
distressed
'That Yoshiko ignored him$_1$ distressed Taro$_1$.'

(Sells 1987a: 461)

In this case, *Taroo* acts as the SELF (and also as the PIVOT).

The 3POV environment is not defined on the basis of the choice of a predicate. It refers to a context where the external speaker chooses to adopt the perspective of an internal protagonist and describes the state of affairs from that protagonist's point of view. In this case, the external speaker bears the SOURCE and SELF roles, while the internal protagonist is the PIVOT.

(89) Japanese
Takasi₁-wa [Yosiko-ga zibun₁-o tazunete-kita node]
Takashi-TOP Yoshiko-NOM self-ACC visit-came because
kanasigar-anakat-ta.
become.sad-NEG-PAST
'Takashi₁ was not sad because Yoshiko came to visit him₁.'
(Sells 1987a: 472)

Notice that not all logically possible combinations of role specifications are claimed to exist, as is clear from Table 2.1. Rather, it can be seen that there is an implicational hierarchy; that is, if SOURCE is internal, then so are SELF and PIVOT, and if SELF is internal, then so is PIVOT (Sells 1987a: 456). Incidentally, in direct speech contexts (or non-logophoric contexts), all roles are associated with the external speaker.

According to Sells, languages differ with respect to which role is allowed to antecede a logophoric expression. For example, PIVOT qualifies as an antecedent for Japanese *zibun* but not for Icelandic *sig*. The following Icelandic sentence is not acceptable precisely because the intended antecedent for *sig* is understood as the PIVOT.

(90) Icelandic
*Jón₁ er hér enn þó að María kyssi sig₁.
Jon is here still although Maria kisses.SBJ self
(Sells 1987a: 473)

We have seen that discourse factors play important roles in determining the antecedence of logophors, and the interaction of these factors gives rise to variation in logophoric phenomena. Sells's taxonomy of logocentric antecedents makes it clear that just as languages restrict the range of possible logophoric domains in accordance with certain implicational hierarchies, the range of logocentric antecedents permitted in a given language is determined in some similar fashion. For example, Japanese allows binding of *zibun* by a PIVOT, which in turn predicts that it also allows *zibun*-binding by a SOURCE or a SELF.

2.4. Antilogophoricity

At the opposite end of the spectrum from logophoricity lies antilogophoricity, but unlike the former, little is known about the latter for reasons that will become clear as our investigation unfolds.

As the name implies, antilogophoricity refers to a phenomenon wherein an expression is forced to be disjoint from the logophoric center in a given context. Thus, in normal cases, the referent of the antecedent of an antilogophor needs to be distinct from the individual whose speech, thoughts, or feelings are being reported.

To give an example, it has been claimed that English epithets have antilogophoric properties (Narahara 1991; Dubinsky and Hamilton 1998). They exhibit disjoint-reference effects when their antecedent is the one whose speech, thoughts, or feelings are being reported.

(91) *John$_1$ thinks that the idiot$_1$ will win.

(92) *He$_1$ told Naomi that the bastard$_1$ was going to visit his grandfather.

For example, in (91), *the idiot* cannot refer to *John* because it is John's perspective in terms of which the embedded report is made. Similarly, in (92) *he* and *the bastard* cannot be coreferent because *he* is the individual from whose point of view the embedded proposition is reported.

The idea that epithets are antilogophoric is supported by the fact that they can refer to an individual who is not understood as the agent of reported speech or thought. Some examples are given below.

(93) My brother$_1$ invests in many projects that the idiot$_1$ thinks will make him rich.

(Haïk 1984: 204, fn21)

(94) The teenager$_1$ rode the motorcycle which the brat$_1$ got as a birthday gift.

(Narahara 1991: 48)

(95) John$_1$ has proven by this incident that I cannot trust the idiot$_1$.

(Narahara 1991: 66)

(96) I introduced John₁ to a woman whom the idiot₁ had been wanting to meet.

(Narahara 1991: 66)

(97) John₁ has no idea how much trouble the bastard₁ caused me.

(Narahara 1991: 77)

(98) John₁ ran over a man (who was) trying to give the idiot₁ directions.

(Dubinsky and Hamilton 1998: 688)

(99) Through an accumulation of slipups, John₁ (inadvertently) led his students to conclude that the idiot₁ couldn't teach.

(Dubinsky and Hamilton 1998: 688)

As we will discuss in more detail in subsequent chapters, it is usually very difficult to detect antilogophoricity because the effects of antilogophoricity restrictions tend to be concealed by or masquerade as other independent phenomena. This is why antilogophoricity is far less documented or discussed than logophoricity, despite the fact that its existence was hinted at as early as Kuno (1972).

2.5. Binding vs. Coreference (Covaluation)

Before moving on, it is perhaps appropriate to discuss two distinct mechanisms of establishing anaphoric relations. A widely accepted view is that a pronoun can be anaphorically related to its antecedent in at least two ways. On this view, intrasentential anaphora can be obtained either via a process called *coreference* (or more broadly, *covaluation*) or via *variable binding* (or *binding* for short). That is, a pronoun may corefer with a DP by picking up the same reference as that DP, or alternatively, it can function as a variable bound by some operator. The former type of anaphoric relation is called coreference, whereas the latter type is called binding. In the following sentence, for instance, *he* can be anaphoric to *John* in two different ways, as roughly represented in (101).[7]

---

[7] An assignment g is a function from the set of natural numbers to individuals.

(100) John thinks he is smart.

(101) a. *Coreference*
John (λx (x thinks he$_1$ is smart))   g(1) = John
  b. *Binding*
John (λx (x thinks x is smart))

In the case of (101a), the pronoun, as a free variable, picks up the referential value *John* from the relevant inventory of discourse entities, whereas in the case of (101b), the pronoun is bound by the lambda operator.[8] While there are apparently no discernible differences in meaning between (101a) and (101b), it has been reported that the two construals are empirically distinguished under ellipsis contexts (Keenan 1971; Sag 1976; Williams 1977, among others).

(102) John thinks he is smart, and Bill does too.

The second conjunct in the above sentence, which involves an elided VP, can be interpreted in two ways. Under the so-called strict reading, it means that Bill thinks John is smart, whereas under the so-called sloppy reading, it means that Bill thinks Bill himself is smart. The ambiguity here is straightforwardly explained in terms of the difference between coreference and binding. That is, if the elided VP contains a coreferential pronoun (as in (103a)), it receives a strict interpretation because the referential value of the pronoun is fixed once and for all in the first conjunct, whereas if the elided VP contains a variable, the pronoun must be linked to the relevant binder, which gives rise to a sloppy interpretation, as in (103b).

(103) a. Bill (λx (x thinks he$_1$ is smart))   g(1) = John
   b. Bill (λx (x thinks x is smart))

The two types of anaphoric interpretation can also be distinguished by using the focus particle *only*. For example, the following sentence carries different entailments, depending on whether the pronoun is interpreted as a coreferential pronoun or a bound variable.

(104) (Of all the women) only Sally thinks that Bill trusts her.

---

[8] On this view, binding is seen as the procedure of closing a property.

(105) a. Sally is the only person who thinks Bill trusts Sally
b. Sally is the only person x such that x thinks Bill trusts x

If the pronoun *her* in (104) corefers with *Sally*, the sentence is interpreted as in (105a), which entails that the other women do not think that Bill trusts Sally. By contrast, if the pronoun *her* in (104) is interpreted as a bound variable, the sentence is interpreted as in (105b) so that it entails that the other women do not think that they are trusted by Bill.

While a pronoun can be anaphorically related to a referential DP either via coreference or binding, it is only a binding relation that can hold between a pronoun and a quantificational antecedent. This is because quantificational expressions do not have reference and therefore cannot enter into a coreference relation with anything.

It is also widely assumed that semantic binding of a pronoun is possible only when the pronoun is c-commanded by its antecedent, whereas such a structural requirement is not necessary for coreference, as exemplified by the contrast between (106c–d), on the one hand, and (107c–d), on the other. (The examples in (106) and (107) are taken from Grodzinsky and Reinhart (1993: 72))

(106) a. Lucie$_1$ adores her$_1$ friends.
b. Alfred$_1$ thinks he$_1$ is a great cook.
c. Most of her$_1$ friends adore Lucie$_1$.
d. A party without Lucie$_1$ annoys her$_1$.

(107) a. Every actress$_1$ adores her$_1$ friends.
b. Every scholar$_1$ thinks he$_1$ is a great cook.
c. *Most of her$_1$ friends adore every actress$_1$.
d. *A party without every actress$_1$ annoys her$_1$.

Under Reinhart's (1983) version of the Binding Theory, Condition B is seen as a restriction on variable binding, and on this view, coreference is not restricted by any of the Binding Conditions. In other words, pronouns are subject to Condition B only when they are interpreted as bound variables.

One might wonder, then, why the pronoun in (108) is not able to corefer with a local referential DP given that coreference (as opposed to variable binding) lies outside the purview of Condition B.

(108) Bill adores him. (*Bill = him)

Building on Reinhart (1983), Grodzinsky and Reinhart (1993) propose that what blocks intrasentential coreference in cases like (108) is not a syntactic principle but an economy condition called *Rule I*.

(109) *Rule I: Intrasentential Coreference*
NP A cannot corefer with NP B if replacing A with C, C a variable A-bound by B, yields an indistinguishable interpretation.
(Grodzinsky and Reinhart 1993: 79)

Rule I ensures that accidental coreference is possible just in case the coreference construal is not equivalent to the interpretation that would be obtained by binding. While there are several versions of Rule I that have been proposed in the literature (see, for example, Reinhart (2006) and Roelofsen (2010) for extensive discussion), the precise formulation of this principle is not important for our purposes here. The point is that in (108), replacing *him*, at LF, with an A-bound variable results in the representation *Bill (λx (x adores x))*, which is indistinguishable from the coreference interpretation where *Bill* and *him* are assigned the same value. Rule I thus precludes the coreference option in (108).

In normal contexts, then, Rule I basically achieves the same results as can be obtained by Chomsky's (1981, 1986) version of the Binding Theory, where binding and coreference are uniformly regulated in the syntax. However, there are cases in which coreference is allowed even in Condition B environments (namely, where a pronoun has a local antecedent). For instance, the sentence in (110) below allows the pronoun *him* to corefer with the local referential DP *Bill*.

(110) I know what Bill and Mary have in common. Mary adores Bill and Bill adores him too.
(adapted from Reinhart 1983: 169)

Contrary to what is predicted by Chomsky's version of the Binding Theory, the pronoun *him* can be coreferential with the local subject *Bill* in this sentence. Under Reinhart's version, by contrast, the well-formedness of the sentence receives a straightforward explanation; in this context, the bound-variable interpretation of *him* is not identical to the intended coreference reading. To be more specific, what the speaker intends to assert in (110) is that both Mary and Bill have the property of adoring Bill, rather than the property of being a self-adorer. Since the coreference interpretation (i.e., (111a) below) is not equivalent to the reading that would be obtained by variable binding (i.e., (111b)), Rule I does not preempt intrasentential coreference here.

(111) a. *Coreference*
Bill (λx (x adores him$_6$)) $g(6) =$ Bill
b. *Binding*
Bill (λx (x adores x))

Importantly, this is in stark contrast with a bound (as opposed to referential) pronoun, which is not allowed to have a local antecedent regardless of context. For example, under no circumstances does the following sentence allow the pronoun to take the local subject *every boy* as its antecedent.

(112)   Every boy adores him.

Since, in this case, coreference is not an option to start with (precisely because quantified expressions do not refer), the sentence is outright ungrammatical due to Condition B, and Rule I is simply irrelevant here.

It may incidentally be noted that in some restricted cases, the bound-variable/coreference ambiguity shows up even when the antecedent of the pronoun is quantificational.[9] It has therefore been suggested that coreference is subsumed under a more general mechanism called *covaluation* (see Reinhart 2000, 2006; Roelofsen 2010; cf. Heim 1998 for relevant discussion).

To avoid unnecessary confusion and complication, I will use the traditional term "coreference" because the distinction between coreference and covaluation is orthogonal to the discussion in the present study.

---

[9] For example, *Every wife thinks that only she respects her husband* may entail either that every wife thinks that the other wives do not respect their own husband, or that every wife thinks that the other wives do not respect her husband (see Heim 1998; Reinhart 2000, 2006; Roelofsen 2010).

Chapter 3

Concealed Antilogophoricity: A Case Study of Japanese Pronominal Binding

3.1. Overt third-person pronouns in Japanese

This chapter presents a case study of the Japanese overt third-person pronouns *kare* 'he' and *kanozyo* 'she', which pose difficult challenges for the Binding Theory. At first sight, it seems that they are constrained in the same way as English pronouns. As demonstrated below, local binding and coreference are prohibited.

(1) a. ?*Taroo$_1$-wa kare$_1$-o hometa.
    Taro-TOP he-ACC praised
    'Taro praised him.'
  b. ?*Hanako$_1$-wa kanozyo$_1$-o hometa.
    Hanako-TOP she-ACC praised
    'Hanako praised her.'

(2) *Dono-gakusei$_1$-mo kare$_1$/kanozyo$_1$-o hometa.
    every-student-PART he/she-ACC praised
    'Every student praised him/her.'

If we look at non-local binding/coreference possibilities, however, a peculiar pattern emerges. It has been reported that *kare* and *kanozyo* can be anaphor-

47

ically related to an antecedent via coreference but not via binding (Kitagawa 1981; Saito and Hoji and 1983; Sportiche 1986; Hoji, 1990, 1991; Noguchi 1995, 1997; Déchaine and Wiltschko 2002, among others).[1] In other words, they can refer but cannot function as bound variables, as the contrast between (3) and (4) demonstrates.

(3) Taroo$_1$-wa kare$_{1/2}$-ga katu to omotteiru.
Taro-TOP he-NOM win COMP think
'Taro thinks that he will win.'

(4) Dono-gakusei$_1$-mo kare$_{*1/2}$-ga katu to omotteiru.
every-student-PART he-NOM win COMP think
'Taro thinks that he will win.'

What this suggests is that modulating the definition of locality alone does not seem sufficient to capture the patterns of Japanese pronominal binding under the standard Binding Theory, where binding and coreference are both defined in terms of coindexation (i.e., identity of indices) and are regulated in the same fashion.

Also, the data pose a learnability problem if we suppose that children initially entertain the hypothesis that pronouns can be used as either free or bound variables. In other words, if pronouns of the English type are the default option, the unbindability of Japanese third-person pronouns could not be learned on the basis of positive evidence directly available to Japanese-speaking children.

There are several ways to address this learnability issue. One possible line of approach is to claim that children come equipped with the knowledge that pronouns of the Japanese type are the default (see Sportiche 1986: 374 for discussion). Note that this is not a logically forced move. Such an approach is based on the tacit assumption that children are only attentive to direct evidence to acquire relevant linguistic knowledge. This assumption, which Pearl and Mis (2012) call the *direct evidence assumption*, is by no means self-evident.

Another conceivable way to solve this puzzle, therefore, is to hypoth-

---

[1] As we will see later, these pronouns can in fact be bound in certain restricted contexts.

esize that children use indirect evidence to converge on the correct knowledge of these pronouns. For instance, learners may employ a probabilistic learning strategy drawing indirect evidence from, say, the properties of other pronominal elements in the same language. In the case of Japanese, it is not implausible that Japanese-speaking children learn the relevant anaphoric properties of *kare/kanozyo* indirectly from the distributional data of the anaphor *zibun* 'self'.

Still another possibility is that there is evidence, whether direct or indirect, that suggests that these putative pronouns are characterized as something other than genuine pronouns and are therefore not constrained in the same way as pronouns.

In order to answer the question of how Japanese-speaking children come to know the anaphoric patterns of overt third-person pronouns, it is crucial to address the question of what determines the binding-theoretic properties of these elements because the answer to the first question hinges ultimately on the answer to the second.[2]

In what follows, we will first take a look at the basic properties of overt third-person pronouns in Japanese, and review previous approaches to the putative unbindability of third-person pronouns in Japanese. We will then look at the recent observations made by Hoji et al. (2000) and Hara (2002), which, contrary to the widely held assumption, suggest that Japanese third-person pronouns can actually function as bound variables under certain restricted environments. The central question that will be addressed, therefore, is why third-person pronouns in Japanese can be bound only in a subset of the contexts in which third-person pronouns in languages like English can be bound. I will show that antilogophoricity is operative behind the scenes in determining the distribution and interpretation of *kare/kanozyo*.

---

[2] There are other important issues pertaining to children's pronoun interpretation. One issue, known as the delay of Principle B effect (DPBE), is concerned with the well-known observation that children apparently fail to show knowledge of Condition B. For an in-depth overview of previous studies on the DPBE, see Conroy et al. (2009). Another issue is concerned with children's apparent inability to compute the Avoid Pronoun Principle. See Shibata and Yashima (2014) for discussion.

3.2. Basic Facts

Let us begin by looking at the basic properties of third-person pronouns in Japanese. It seems safe to say that overt third-person pronouns in Japanese (such as *kare* 'he' and *kanozyo* 'she') display a full range of properties that are typically associated with referential (as opposed to bound) pronouns.

First of all, *kare* and *kanozyo* can take a non-local referential antecedent regardless of whether they are c-commanded by the antecedent (Kanzaki 1994: 125 and references therein), as the following examples demonstrate.

(5) a. Taroo$_1$-wa Hanako-ga kare$_1$-o nikundeiru to omotteiru.
    Taro-TOP Hanako-NOM he-ACC hate COMP think
    'Taro thinks that Hanako hates him.'

   b. Hanako$_1$-wa Taroo-ga kanozyo$_1$-o nikundeiru to omotteiru.
    Hanako-TOP Taro-NOM she-ACC hate COMP think
    'Hanako thinks that Taro hates her.'

(6) a. Izen kare$_1$-o nikundeita hito-ga Taroo$_1$-o tasuketa.
    before he-ACC hated person-NOM Taro-ACC helped
    'The person who used to hate him helped Taro.'

   b. Izen kanozyo$_1$-o nikundeita hito-ga Hanako$_1$-o tasuketa.
    before she-ACC hated person-NOM Hanako-ACC helped
    'The person who used to hate her helped Hanako.'

Secondly, just like English referential pronouns, Japanese overt third-person pronouns normally resist having a local referential antecedent but are allowed to have one under appropriate contexts (Hoji 1995; cf. Reinhart 1983), while they cannot have local quantified antecedents under any circumstances.[3]

---

[3] As mentioned in Chapter 2, the underlying idea here is that as opposed to variable binding, which is regulated by Binding Conditions, coreference is governed by an economy condition called Rule I (Grodzinsky and Reinhart 1993; Reinhart 2006; Reinhart 1983), which blocks accidental coreference if the coreference interpretation is equivalent to what would be obtained by binding.

(7) a. #Taroo$_1$-ga kare$_1$-o nikundeiru.
    Taro-NOM he-ACC hate
    'Taro hates him.'
  b. *Dono gakusei$_1$-mo kare$_1$-o nikundeiru.
    every student-PART he-ACC hate
    'Every student hates him.'

Thirdly, as reported by Saito and Hoji (1983: 257), no sloppy reading is available in sentences of the following sort.

(8) (Subeteno dansi gakusei nonakade) Taroo-dake-ga Hanako-ga
    all   male student among   Taro-only-NOM Hanako-NOM
    kare-o uttaeru to   omotteiru.
    he-ACC sue   COMP think
    '(Of all male students) only Taro thinks Hanako will sue him.'

Disregarding any readings where the pronoun refers to someone other than Taro, the above sentence has only one interpretation. Crucially, it has the reading (9a), but (9b) is not a possible interpretation for (8).

(9) a. [Only x: x = Taro] x thinks Hanako will sue him$_2$ $g(2)$ = Taro
  b. [Only x: x = Taro] x thinks Hanako will sue x

This means that sentence (8) entails that the other male students do not think that Hanako will sue Taro, but does not entail that the other male students do not think that they will be sued by Hanako. This is confirmed by the fact that the statement in (8) can be denied by uttering the sentence in (10a), whereas the sentence in (10b) is not a felicitous denial of the statement.

(10) a. Iya, boku-mo Hanako-ga   Taroo/kare-o uttaeru to
     No I-also   Hanako-NOM Taro/he-ACC sue   COMP
     omotteiru.
     think
     'No, I also think Hanako will sue Taro/him.'
   b. Iya, boku-mo Hanako-ga   boku-o uttaeru to   omotteiru.
     No I-also   Hanako-NOM I-ACC sue   COMP think
     'No, I also think Hanako will sue me.'

These observations indicate that like English referential pronouns, Japanese overt third-person pronouns can at least enter into coreference relations with referential antecedents.

However, the absence of a sloppy interpretation for (8) seems puzzling in view of the fact that the English counterpart to (8), given below as (11), allows both strict and sloppy readings.

(11) Only Taro thinks that Hanako will sue him.

Not only the absence of sloppy readings but also other facts suggest that Japanese overt third-person pronouns do not pattern with English bound pronouns. For example, overt third-person pronouns in Japanese fail to give rise to bound-variable readings even in those environments where they are c-commanded by a non-local quantificational DP.

(12) a. ?*Dono gakusei$_1$-mo kare$_1$-ga isya-ni naru to sinziteiru.
every student-PART he-NOM doctor-as become COMP believe
'Every student believes that he will become a doctor.'
b. ?*Dono gakusei$_1$-mo Hanako-ga kare$_1$-o tasukeru to
every student-PART Hanako-NOM he-ACC help COMP
omotteiru.
think
'Every student thinks that Hanako will help him.'
c. ?*Dono gakusei$_1$-ga kare$_1$-ga saihu-o nakusita to
which student-NOM he-NOM wallet-ACC lost COMP
itta-no?
said-Q
'Which student said that he lost his wallet?'

Thus, it has often been claimed that unlike their English counterparts, Japanese overt third-person pronouns such as *kare* 'he' and *kanozyo* 'she' cannot be interpreted as bound variables (Kitagawa 1981; Saito and Hoji 1983; Sportiche 1986; Hoji 1990, 1991; Noguchi 1995, 1997; Déchaine and Wiltschko 2002, among others). For example, the sentence in (13) has an interpretation in which the third-person pronoun *kare* refers to some individual whose reference is understood in the context, but does not have an interpretation in which the pronoun is bound by the quantificational DP *dono gakusei(-mo)* 'every student' (as represented in (14)).

(13) Dono gakusei-mo kare-ga katu to omotteiru.
every student-PART he-NOM win COMP think
'Every student thinks that he will win.'

(14) every student (λx (x thinks x will win))

In order to express the interpretation given in (14), *zibun* 'self' or a null pronoun needs to be used instead of *kare*.

(15) Dono gakusei$_1$-mo {zibun$_1$-ga/ø$_1$} katu to omotteiru.
every student-PART self-NOM win COMP think
'Every student thinks that he will win.'

These observations led many researchers to the following generalization:

(16) Overt third-person pronouns in Japanese can only refer.

Over the last few decades, various analyses have been proposed to account for this seemingly peculiar property of Japanese overt third-person pronouns (Montalbetti 1984; Sportiche 1986; Hoji 1990, 1991; Katada 1991; Aoun and Hornstein 1992; Noguchi 1995, 1997; Déchaine and Wiltschko 2002). As we will see, however, the generalization stated in (16) is only apparent; there are cases in which *kare* and *kanozyo* can be construed as bound variables. This means that the previous analyses just cited are inadequate to capture the true nature of Japanese personal pronouns, as they rest on the false premise that overt third-person pronouns in Japanese cannot be bound. That said, since all these analyses offer some insightful ideas, it is worthwhile to review them first.

3.3. The (Putative) "Unbindability" of Overt Third-Person Pronouns: Previous Studies

3.3.1. Sportiche (1986)

This section reviews Sportiche (1986), who attempts to capture the properties of the Japanese third-person pronoun *kare* in association with the properties of the reflexive *zibun*.

Sportiche's analysis is based on the idea that pronouns (including anaphors) are characterized along two dimensions, namely whether they require a c-commanding antecedent (i.e., binder) and whether they are subject to a locality condition or an anti-locality condition. In English, an anaphor requires a binder in the same sentence, and it is also subject to a locality constraint. Pronouns, on the other hand, are divided into two types. One type, which we call *him*$_{[-R]}$ for convenience, functions as a bound variable and as such requires a c-commanding antecedent. The other type, which we call *him*$_{[+R]}$, is a pronoun used referentially, and it does not require a binder. Both types of pronouns are subject to an anti-locality constraint, meaning that pronouns, either free or bound variables, must be disjoint from c-commanding DPs in the same domain. The English pronominal system is therefore summarized as follows.

(17) *English Pronominal System*

lexical item	requires a binder	subject to a locality [+]/ anti-locality [−] constraint
himself	+	+
him [−R]	+	−
him [+R]	−	−

Let us now turn to the Japanese pronominal system. Just like English reflexives, the Japanese reflexive *zibun* must be bound. However, it differs from English anaphors in that it can be bound either locally or non-locally.

(18) Taroo$_1$-wa zibun$_1$-o suisensita.
Taro-TOP self-ACC recommended
'Taro recommended himself.'

(19) Taroo$_1$-wa Hanako$_2$-ga zibun$_{1/2}$-o suisensuru koto-o
Taro-TOP Hanako-NOM self-ACC recommend COMP-ACC
sitteiru.
know
'Taro knows that Hanako will recommend him/herself.'

In a sense, then, *zibun* acts as either a local anaphor or a bound pronoun. For convenience, we call the former use of *zibun* *zibun*$_{[+L]}$ and the latter use *zibun*$_{[-L]}$.

In contrast to *zibun*, third-person pronouns in Japanese can only be used referentially and cannot be bound (so it was believed by a number of researchers including, among others, Kitagawa (1981) and Saito and Hoji (1983)).

(20) Taroo$_1$-wa kare$_1$-ga yuusyoosuru to omotteiru.
Taro-TOP he-NOM win.first.prize COMP think
'Taro thinks that he will win first prize.'

(21) Dono gakusei$_1$-mo kare$_{*1}$/zibun$_1$-ga yuusyoosuru to
every student-PART he/self-NOM win.first.prize COMP
omotteiru.
think
'Every student thinks that he will win first prize.'

In other words, the third-person pronoun *kare* corresponds to a referential pronoun (i.e., *him*$_{[+R]}$) in English. The Japanese pronominal system is summarized as follows.

(22) *Japanese Pronominal System*

lexical item	requires a binder	subject to a locality [+]/ anti-locality [−] constraint
zibun [+L]	+	+
zibun [−L]	+	−
kare	−	−

These observations suggest that English and Japanese have essentially the same pronominal system, and the superficial differences are attributed to the differences in the way pronominal elements are lexicalized. To be more specific, English lexically distinguishes between those which must be locally bound and those which must be locally free, whereas Japanese lexically distinguishes between referentially defective pronouns (i.e., bound variables) and referentially independent pronouns. If so, the seemingly peculiar properties of *kare* are not so surprising when viewed from the overall system of anaphoric reference in Japanese.

Under Sportiche's analysis, the binding-theoretic differences between English and Japanese pronouns are, in effect, accidental. On this view, the reason that *kare* resists variable binding is that it is lexicalized as an exclusively referential pronoun by virtue of the fact that *zibun* happens to be lexicalized in such a way that it acts either as a local anaphor or as a bound pronoun. While this analysis can be seen as a restrictive theory of parametric variation in possible pronoun/anaphor types, it does not resolve the fundamental question of why *kare* must be lexicalized the way it is.

3.3.2. Aoun and Hornstein (1992) and Katada (1991)

Aoun and Hornstein's (1992) point of departure is the idea that there are two distinct anti-locality conditions that pronouns must obey. They argue that one condition requires that a pronoun be A-free in the relevant domain, and the other requires that a pronoun be A'-free in the relevant domain. In the case of English, the domain in which pronouns must be A-free happens to be the same as the domain in which they must be A'-free, and this masks the fact that there are two distinct anti-locality conditions.

In Japanese, on the other hand, pronouns must be A-free in the minimal CFC and A'-free anywhere. Hence the contrast between (23) and (24).

(23) Taroo$_1$-wa kare$_1$-ga yuusyoosuru to omotteiru.
Taro-TOP he-NOM win.first.prize COMP think
'Taro thinks that he will win first prize.'

(24) Dono gakusei$_1$-mo kare$_{*1/2}$-ga yuusyoosuru to omotteiru.
every student-PART he-NOM win.first.prize COMP think
'Every student thinks that he will win first prize.'

In (23), the antecedent of *kare* is *Taroo*, which is in A-position. Since *kare* is A-free in the minimal CFC, the sentence is grammatical. In (24), however, the antecedent of *kare* is the quantificational expression *dono gakusei(-mo)* "every student", which undergoes QR to an A'-position. The LF representation of (24) is given as follows:

(25) [$_{TP}$ Dono-gakusei-mo$_i$ [$_{TP}$ t_i [$_{CP}$ kare-ga yuusyoosuru to] omotteiru]]

Thus, at LF, *dono gakusei(-mo)* A'-binds *kare*, in violation of the anti-locality requirement.

A caveat is in order here. Aoun and Hornstein (1992) assume that the c-command requirement for pronominal binding "must hold between the QP and the pronoun and not necessarily between the variable and the pronoun" (p. 3), unlike the standard view that a pronoun can be interpreted as bound by a quantificational phrase only if it is c-commanded by the variable bound by that QP. Under Aoun and Hornstein's approach, then, weak crossover effects must be accounted for independently. Also, Noguchi (1995, 1997) argues against Aoun and Hornstein's analysis, based on the observation that *kare* can be anteceded by a scrambled phrase. The following example is taken from Noguchi (1997: 773, fn. 3).

(26) John-o$_i$ kare-no hahaoya-ga [keisatu-ga t$_i$ taiho-suru
John-ACC he-GEN mother-NOM police-NOM   arrest-do
daroo to]   omotteiru.
will COMP think
'John, his mother thinks that the police will arrest him.'

Given that (long-distance) scrambling involves A'-movement, it is predicted that in (26), *John-o* cannot antecede *kare*, but the sentence is fine even when the pronoun is coreferential with the scrambled antecedent. Noguchi takes this fact as evidence suggesting that Aoun and Hornstein's analysis is too strong.

To be fair, though, the grammaticality of (26) does not necessarily undermine Aoun and Hornstein's account. It is true that long-distance scrambling shows A'-movement properties, but given that long-distance scrambling is subject to obligatory LF reconstruction (Saito 1992), *kare* in (26) is, after all, A'-free at LF, where the relevant anti-locality requirement is supposed to hold. Perhaps a more compelling piece of evidence against Aoun and Hornstein's claim comes from Abe's (1992) observation, to which we will return shortly.

We have so far looked at two approaches that attempt to capture the binding-theoretic properties of third-person pronouns in Japanese. The two proposals differ in that under Sportiche's approach, the putative unbindabity of *kare* follows from the intrinsic lexical properties of *kare*, whereas under Aoun and Hornstein's approach, it follows from the anti-locality condition on A'-binding.

An advantage, so it is claimed, of Aoun and Hornstein's analysis is that it can provide a principled account of the observation that *kare* must be free not only from quantifiers but also from the reflexive *zibun* (Lasnik 1989).

(27) John-wa [zibun-ga kare-no hahaoya-o semeta to] itta.
John-TOP self-NOM he-GEN mother-ACC blamed COMP said
'John said that he blamed his mother.'
(*kare = John)

In this sentence, *kare* must be disjoint in reference from *John*. Replacing *zibun* with a null pronoun or the overt third-person pronoun *kare* makes coreference between *John* and *kare* possible.[4] (To make sure that the subject *John* in (28a) resides in the matrix clause, it is marked with the topic marker -*wa*, which can occur only in a root clause.)

(28) a. John-wa [φ kare-no hahaoya-o semeta to] itta.
John-TOP he-GEN mother-ACC blamed COMP said
'John said that he killed his mother.'
b. John-wa [kare-ga kare-no hahaoya-o semeta to] itta.
John-TOP he-NOM he-GEN mother-ACC blamed COMP said
'John said that he killed his mother.'

The grammaticality of (28a–b) above suggests that it is the presence of *zibun* that is responsible for the disjoint-reference effect. Yet it is not immediately obvious why *kare* must be disjoint from *zibun*, given that *zibun* is not a quantifier.

At this point, it is perhaps instructive to touch on Katada's (1991) analysis of *zibun*. Katada proposes that *zibun* should be analyzed as what she dubs an *operator anaphor*. Operator anaphors share certain semantic characteristics with standard operators such as quantifiers (including *wh*-phrases) and null operators (see Katada 1991 for details). She claims that just like standard operators, the operator anaphor *zibun* undergoes raising to an A'-position at LF.[5] If Katada is right in claiming that *zibun* moves to an A'-position at LF, the fact that *kare* cannot be bound in (27) follows directly from Aoun and Hornstein's idea that *kare* must be A'-free. Note that as expected, the following sentence (taken from Katada (1991: ex. 54)) allows

---

[4] The sentence in (28b) sounds less natural than (28a) presumably due to an independent economy/pragmatic principle favoring a more attenuated anaphoric form over a less attenuated one. See Section 3.3.6.

[5] The idea of raising anaphors at LF itself is reminiscent of Lebeaux (1983) and Chomsky (1986).

kare and *zibun* to have the same referential value.

(29) John$_1$-ga [kare$_1$-ga Bill$_2$-ni zibun$_{1/*2}$-no koto-o   hanasita
     John-NOM   he-NOM   Bill-DAT self-GEN   matter-ACC told
     to]   omotteiru.
     COMP   think
     'John thinks that he told Bill about him.'

At LF, *zibun* adjoins to the embedded VP to take *kare* as its antecedent. The antecedent of *kare* is *John*, which stays in A-position throughout the derivation. Since *kare* is A'-free, the sentence is grammatical.

The supposed appeal of Aoun and Hornstein's analysis shrivels upon closer scrutiny, however. As pointed out by Abe (1992), it incorrectly predicts that the following sentence is ruled out as ungrammatical.

(30) Masao$_1$-wa [[kare$_1$-ga sukidatta sensei]-ga   zibun$_1$-o nikundeiru
     Masao-TOP   he-NOM   liked   teacher-NOM self-ACC   hate
     to]   itta.
     COMP   said
     'Masao said that the teacher he liked hated him.'

If, as Aoun and Hornstein (1992) and Katada (1991) assume, *zibun* raises to an A'-position in order to get locally bound by its antecedent, the above sentence should have the following LF representation.

(31) Masao$_1$ [$_{VP}$ zibun$_1$ [$_{VP}$ [$_{CP}$ [$_{DP}$ kare$_1$ ...] t$_1$ ...] ...]]

Since, in this case, *zibun* moves all the way to the matrix VP, it ends up in an A'-position c-commanding *kare*. The sentence is predicted to be ungrammatical, as *kare* is not A'-free, but it is actually grammatical.

Then it must be concluded that either Aoun and Hornstein's (1992) analysis of *kare* or the A'-movement analysis of *zibun* is false. At any rate, the sentence in (27), repeated here as (32), does not lend any additional support to Aoun and Hornstein's proposal.

(32) John-ga   [zibun-ga   kare-no hahaoya-o   semeta to]   itta.
     John-NOM   self-NOM   he-GEN mother-ACC blamed COMP said
     'John said that he blamed his mother.'
     (*kare* = John)

3.3.3. Montalbetti (1984)

Montalbetti (1984) attempts to derive the unbindability of Japanese personal pronouns from the Overt Pronoun Constraint (OPC), which is claimed to be operative at LF.

(33) *Overt Pronoun Constraint (OPC)*
 Overt pronouns cannot link to formal variables iff the alternation overt/empty obtains.

(Montalbetti 1984: 94)

A "formal variable" here is defined as follows (see Higginbotham 1983).

(34) *Formal Variable*
 v is a formal variable iff (i) v is an empty category in an argument position; and (ii) v is linked to a lexical operator in a non-argument position.

For our purposes here, it is safe to assume that a formal variable is a trace left by *wh*-movement or QR.

Under Montalbetti's analysis, the following contrast is nicely captured.

(35) a. *Dono gakusei$_1$-mo kare$_1$-ga katu to omotteiru.
 every student-PART he-NOM win COMP think
 'Every student thinks that he will win.'
 b. Dono gakusei$_1$-mo ø$_1$ katu to omotteiru.
 every student-PART win COMP think
 'Every student thinks that he will win.'

The OPC-based account correctly predicts that the overt pronoun *kare* in (35) cannot be linked to (the trace of) the *wh*-phrase *dono gakusei(-mo)* 'every student' while the empty pronoun ø in the same position can.

Upon closer scrutiny, however, there are disparities in the behavior of overt pronouns in Japanese and Spanish, the latter of which originally motivated the postulation of the OPC. Specifically, Japanese displays stronger OPC effects than Spanish in the sense that in the latter, the OPC can be circumvented in the presence of an intervening silent pronoun, whereas in the former, it cannot. In languages like Spanish, it is observed that in those configurations where an intermediate bound null pronoun intervenes between a formal variable and an overt pronoun, the binding of the overt pronoun to the formal variable becomes possible. In such syntactic contexts, the intermediate bound *pro* acts as a mediator between the formal variable and the overt pronoun, which is schematically represented as follows.

(36) QP/wh-phrase$_i$ [t$_i$ ... [ø ... [overt pronoun ...]]]

However, the same does not apply to Japanese, as Montalbetti observes. Consider the following example.

(37) *Dono gakusei$_1$-mo [$_{CP}$ ø [$_{CP}$ kanarazu kare$_1$-ga katu to] itta to] omotteiru.
every student-PART   definitely he-NOM win COMP said COMP think
'Every student thinks that he said that he would definitely win.'

At LF, the sentence in (37) creates the following configuration, but the overt pronoun *kare* cannot be interpreted as a bound variable.

(38) *Dono gakusei-mo$_i$*   [t$_i$ ... [ø ... [kare ...] ...] ...]

To account for this difference, Montalbetti (1984) postulates the following version of the OPC for Japanese.

(39) *OPC-2*
Overt pronouns cannot have formal variables as antecedents.

(Montalbetti 1984: 187)

According to Montalbetti, languages like Japanese are subject to the OPC-2, which prohibits binding of overt pronouns even more stringently than the OPC. However, the OPC-2 is not merely a stipulation but also a restatement of the problem rather than an explanation, as pointed out by Elbourne (2005) (see also Noguchi 1995, 1997 for arguments against the OPC-based account). As such, Montalbetti's idea does not provide a deep analysis of why Japanese overt pronouns are constrained the way they are.

So far we have looked into the properties of Japanese third-person pronouns based on the tacit assumption that *kare* and *kanozyo* are personal pronouns (of the kind found in English). However, some scholars have challenged this assumption, claiming instead that they are something else. Then the question is: What are they?

3.3.4. Japanese Third-Person Pronouns as NPs (Kuroda 1965)

Greenberg's (1963: 96) linguistic universal 42 states that "[a]ll languages have pronominal categories involving at least three persons and two numbers". The assumption that lies behind this generalization is that all languages have pronouns. However, this is not self-evident when we consider languages like Japanese, namely, languages in which the demarcation between what we label as pronouns and common nouns is not as clear as in Western languages. That is to say, unlike in English, where the three types of nominal expressions (i.e., anaphors, non-reflexive pronouns, and R-expressions) are normally distinguishable based on morphosyntactic criteria, it is not so easy to identify the type of nominal expression in languages like Japanese. Thus, in discussing binding-theoretic phenomena in such languages, it is important to ask whether pronouns constitute a class of forms that should be distinguished from the category of nouns. This issue is indeed a matter of much debate in Japanese linguistics, and no solid consensus has yet been reached.

It should be noted that Japanese does have words that are semantically analogous to English personal pronouns. Some examples are given below.

(40) watasi 'I/me'
anata 'you'
kare 'he/him'
kanozyo 'she/her'
watasitati 'we/us'
anatatati 'you (plural)'
karera 'they/them'

These forms are commonly used when English personal pronouns are translated into Japanese, but the question being addressed here is whether they are distinct from nouns in syntactically/morphologically relevant ways. The purpose of this section is to evaluate the hypothesis that Japanese third-person pronouns are characterized as NPs. We will first take a look at the evidence that has been cited in support of the claim that Japanese third-person pronouns pattern with common nouns rather than bona fide pronouns. Then it will be shown that although Japanese pronouns exhibit apparently noun-like properties, they should nevertheless be separated from common nouns.

Let us first review some of the arguments that have been put forward in favor of the view that Japanese personal pronouns are equivalent to nouns. Kuroda (1965: 105) observes that in Japanese, so-called pronouns can be modified by adjectives, unlike English personal pronouns, which are usually incompatible with adjectival modification. The contrast between (41a-b), on the one hand, and (42a-b), on the other, shows that English pronouns cannot be modified by adjectives directly, whereas Japanese readily allows adjectives to modify pronouns that follow them, suggesting that Japanese personal pronouns pattern with noun phrases.

(41) a. the short man
 b. *the short he

(42) a. tiisai hito
 short man
 b. tiisai kare
 short he

Similarly, it is possible to attach a relative clause to a pronoun in Japanese.

(43) [$_{RC}$ kinoo Taroo-ga paatii-ni turetekita] kanozyo
 yesterday Taro-NOM party-to brought she
 (Lit.) 'she, who Taro brought to the party yesterday'

Another piece of evidence for the noun-like nature of Japanese personal pronouns is that first- and second-person pronouns come in many varieties (Kuroda 1965: 123).

(44) a. First person singular:
 watasi, watakusi, ore, temae, boku, etc.
 b. Second person singular:
 anata, kimi, omae, temae, etc.

This suggests that they are open-class elements, and in this respect, they pattern with common nouns, not with pronouns.

Furthermore, in modern standard Japanese, *kare* and *kanozyo* can mean 'boyfriend' and 'girlfriend,' respectively. Noguchi (1997) takes this fact as evidence suggesting that Japanese personal pronouns are lexical (as opposed to functional) categories on a par with common nouns. The underlying idea is that only lexical categories can undergo semantic drift.

Kuroda (1965: 106) further points out that the repetition of so-called pronouns in Japanese is more constrained than that of English pronouns. For example, the following English sentence is perfectly grammatical.

(45) He does his work when he feels like doing it.

The literal Japanese translation of (45), as given below, sounds unnatural if not utterly ungrammatical (under the reading where all instances of *kare* refer to the same person).

(46) %Kare-wa kare-ga kare-no sigoto-o si-tai toki-ni
 he-TOP he-NOM he-GEN work-ACC do-want.to when-PART
 kare-no sigoto-o suru.
 he-GEN work-ACC do
 'He does his work when he feels like doing it.'

Interestingly, this is just as unnatural as the following sentence, where all the instances of *kare* are replaced with a name.

(47) %George-wa George-ga George-no sigoto-o si-tai
 George-TOP George-NOM George-GEN work-ACC do-want.to
 toki-ni George-no sigoto-o suru.
 when-PART George-GEN work-ACC do
 (Lit.) 'George does George's work when George feels like doing George's work.'

Sentences (46) and (47) become most natural if all but the first instance of *kare/George* are unexpressed.

(48) George/Kare-wa sigoto-o si-tai toki-ni sigoto-o suru.
 George/he-TOP work-ACC do-want.to when-PART work-ACC do
 'George/He does his work when he feels like doing it.'

These observations seem to indicate that Japanese personal pronouns pattern with common nouns rather than pronouns. Kuroda (1965) therefore concludes that what we have hitherto referred to as Japanese personal pronouns should be treated as nouns rather pronouns.

Such an analysis is far from implausible, in light of the fact that (the precursors of) third-person pronouns in earlier varieties of English also behaved as nouns. For instance, they did occur with adjectival modifiers just as Japanese third-person pronouns do.[6] Below are some examples from the *OED* collected by Kanzaki (1994: 14) and from Shakespeare's English collected by Abbott (1869: 149).

(49) a. He has shewed as much honesty and bravery of spirit as any *he* in Mansoul.—Bunyan, *Holy War*, 275
 b. He—that great *he*—covers all.—G. Meredith, *The Tragic Comedians*, 230
 c. Her vertues many compare with the proudest *she* that waits vpon your Queen.—Greene, *The Scottish Historie of James the Fourth*, I. iii. 679
 d. For every he has got him a *she*.—*Westminster Drollery*, II. 80
 e. Those are not *shes*—they're both men.—Fenn, *Real Gold*, 40

(50) a. Lady, you are the cruellest *she* alive.—Shakespeare, *Twelfth Night*, i. 5. 259
 b. Betwixt two such *shes*. Shakespeare, *Cymbeline*, i. 6. 40; ib. i. 3. 29

In these examples, *he* and *she* simply seem to mean "man" and "woman", respectively. Both are used as ordinary nouns and are distinct from pronouns, as evidenced by the fact that they can be quantified (as in (49a)), can follow an indefinite article (as in (49d)), can bear regular plural morphology (as in (49e) and (50b)), and fail to show case inflection.[7]

To recap, Kuroda (1965) claims that so-called pronouns in Japanese are

---

[6] It should be noted that in Present-day English, too, pronouns can occur with certain adjectival modifiers (Jespersen 1949: 134; Kanzaki 1994: 13–14; Noguchi 1997: 778), as in *poor me, little you, the real you,* and *another you*. However, expressions of this sort are not productive, and behave rather differently from full-fledged personal pronouns (see Noguchi 1997 for discussion).

[7] A relic of this usage is still found in Present-day English (e.g., *Is it a he or a she?*).

equivalent to nouns. On this view, modern standard Japanese does not have overt personal pronouns, and the closest Japanese counterparts to personal pronouns in Western languages are null pronouns (see also Martin 1975: 1075).

3.3.5. Japanese Pronouns as N-Pronouns (Noguchi 1995, 1997; Déchaine and Wiltschko 2002)

Building mainly on Kuroda's observations, Noguchi (1995, 1997) develops an idea that there are two types of pronouns: D-pronouns (i.e., pronouns that fall under the category of D) and N-pronouns (i.e., pronouns that are morphosyntactically equivalent to nouns). He further claims that only functional items can serve as bound variables, which entails that nouns cannot be bound since they are lexical. Thus, while both D- and N-pronouns can be used as referential pronouns, only the former can be construed as bound variables.

Under Noguchi's classification, English third-person pronouns correspond to D-pronouns, while Japanese third-person pronouns are analyzed as N-pronouns. This morphosyntactic difference, he argues, is responsible for the binding-theoretic differences between the pronouns in these languages. That is, the unbindability of Japanese third-person pronouns is reduced to the general prohibition against binding of lexical categories.

Déchaine and Wiltschko (2002) propose a finer-grained typology of pronouns, according to which pronouns are divided into three types (i.e., pro-DP, pro-ϕP, and pro-NP), each of which is associated with a syntactically distinct projection, as illustrated below.

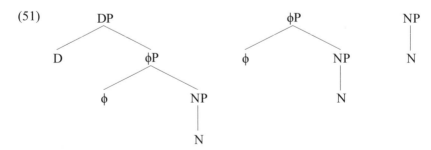

(51)

A pro-DP is composed of three layers of projection. It is syntactically a DP and internally contains a φP and an NP. A φP is a functional projection that is smaller than a DP and larger than an NP. The φ head is considered to be the locus of φ-features. A pro-NP syntactically constitutes an NP.

Just like Noguchi, Déchaine and Wiltschko claim that the morphosyntactic makeup of a given pronoun determines its syntactic distribution and inherent semantics, which in turn determines its binding-theoretic properties. Below is a summary of the properties of each pronoun type.

	Pro-DP	Pro-φP	Pro-NP
Internal syntax	D syntax; morphologically complex	neither D syntax nor N syntax	N syntax
Distribution	argument	argument or predicate	predicate
Semantics	definite	—	constant
Binding-theoretic status	R-expression	variable	—

Table 3.1 Nominal Proform Typology (Déchaine and Wiltschko 2002: 410)

A pro-DP only occurs in argument position. It is classified as an R-expression, thereby falling under Condition C of the Binding Theory. A φP is simply a spell-out of φ-features, and is subject to Condition B. It can function either as an argument or as a predicate. A pro-NP occurs in predicate position. It is semantically a constant and is "undefined with respect to binding theory", which means that its binding-theoretic properties "follow from its inherent semantics" (Déchaine and Wiltschko 2002: 411), a point on which I will elaborate below.

Déchaine and Wiltschko (2002) classify Japanese third-person pronouns as pro-NPs (on the basis of the evidence reported by Kuroda (1965) and Noguchi (1997), which we saw earlier). They attempt to derive the unbindability of these pronouns from the inherent semantics of pro-NPs. That is, since pro-NPs are constants, and since constants cannot function as bound variables, it follows that Japanese third-person pronouns, being pro-NPs, cannot be bound.

While Déchaine and Wiltschko's study has important theoretical implications for the (crosslinguistic) study of pronouns, it has some empirical problems as well. One problem is that their analysis incorrectly predicts that the distribution of third-person pronouns in Japanese is restricted to predicate positions. The following sentences demonstrate that Japanese third-person pronouns can actually show up either in predicate position or in argument position.[8]

(52) a. Sore-wa kare/kanozyo-da.
that-TOP he/she-COP
'That is him/her.'
b. Kare-ga kanozyo-o mita
he-NOM she-ACC saw
'He saw her.'

If we follow Déchaine and Wiltschko's taxonomy, the fact that *kare* and *kanozyo* can appear not only in predicate position but also in argument position forces us to conclude that they are φPs. However, analyzing these pronouns as φPs would undermine the very point of Déchaine and Wiltschko's analysis because their major claim is that the morphosyntactic organization of a given pronoun can be used as a predictor of its binding-theoretic properties.

It is also hard to see how their analysis accounts for the fact that in Condition B environments, Japanese third-person pronouns behave in the same way as pronouns of the English type. As we saw at the beginning of this chapter, *kare* and *kanozyo* resist local binding and coreference alike.

(53) a. ?*Taroo$_1$-wa kare$_1$-o hometa.
Taro-TOP he-ACC praised
'Taro praised him.'
b. ?*Hanako$_1$-wa kanozyo$_1$-o hometa.
Hanako-TOP she-ACC praised
'Hanako praised her.'

(54) *Dono-gakusei$_1$-mo kare$_1$/kanozyo$_1$-o hometa.
every-student-PART he/she-ACC praised
'Every student praised him/her.'

---

[8] Note that it is not entirely clear whether *kare/kanozyo* in (52a) is in predicate position because *kare/kanozyo* does not predicate a property of *sore*. In other words, the copular sentence here is not predicational but identificational. That said, what is crucial here is the fact that *kare* and *kanozyo* can occur in argument position.

Déchaine and Wiltschko (2002: 418) touch on the question of why Japanese personal pronouns are not subject to Condition C, but they fail to discuss why they behave like Condition B pronouns in the local domain.

3.3.6. Japanese Personal Pronouns Are Not NPs

Above we saw a number of facts which purportedly reveal certain commonalities between Japanese personal pronouns and lexical nouns. While it is true that Japanese personal pronouns have properties that are not observed for English personal pronouns, I will now argue that Japanese pronouns are not NPs.

The first piece of evidence against the NP analysis of Japanese personal pronouns comes from the feature specification of the pronouns. The pronoun *kare*, for instance, is specified for gender (i.e., [MALE]) and number (i.e., [SINGULAR]) as well as for person if [3RD PERSON] is assumed to be a linguistically relevant person feature. Déchaine and Wiltschko (2002: fn. 10) note that gender is not necessarily a φ-feature, claiming that the [MALE] feature associated with *kare* is lexical (as opposed to grammatical) gender. However, the number specification of *kare* still remains to be explained. Notice that in this respect, *kare* contrasts sharply with lexical nouns in the same language; that is, in Japanese, common nouns are generally underspecified with respect to number. Take the lexical noun *hito* 'human/person' for example. It can mean a singular individual or a group of people, depending on the context. Thus, the following sentence can mean either 'There is a person in the garden,' or 'There are people in the garden.'

(55) Niwa-ni hito-ga i-ru.
 garden-LOC person-NOM be-PRES
 'There is a person in the garden/There are people in the garden.'

The ambiguity can be resolved by using a numeral quantifier, which again confirms the fact that nouns in Japanese are underspecified with respect to number.

(56) a. Niwa-ni hito-ri-no hito-ga i-ru.
 garden-LOC one-CL-GEN person-NOM be-PRES
 'There is one person in the garden.'

b. Niwa-ni huta-ri-no hito-ga i-ru.
   garden-LOC two-CL-GEN person-NOM be-PRES
   'There are two people in the garden.'
c. Niwa-ni takusan-no hito-ga i-ru.
   garden-LOC many-GEN person-NOM be-PRES
   'There are many people in the garden.'

If, as Déchaine and Wiltschko argue, ϕ-features are encoded by ϕPs, it follows that *kare* must involve a ϕP, which contradicts their own claim that Japanese third-person pronouns are composed solely of NPs.

The second piece of evidence against the NP status of Japanese third-person pronouns comes from the definiteness of these pronouns (cf. Elbourne 2005). Unlike common nouns, which normally receive an indefinite interpretation, *kare* and *kanozyo* obligatorily receive a definite interpretation. Thus, ?**dono-kare*, which literally means 'which he,' is not a possible expression.⁹ This contrasts with, say, *dono-hito* 'which person,' which is a perfectly well-formed phrase. In a similar vein, common nouns, like indefinites, cannot be anaphoric (across sentences) in the absence of a demonstrative determiner, while *kare* and *kanozyo* can. This difference makes sense if we suppose that unlike common nouns, *kare* and *kanozyo* structurally involve a projection that encodes definiteness.

The third piece of counterevidence actually comes from the prima facie evidence cited by Kuroda (1965) and Noguchi (1995, 1997) in support of the claim that Japanese personal pronouns are nouns (or N-pronouns). Recall that Japanese personal pronouns can be modified by prenominal adjectives or relative clauses—a fact that Kuroda (1965) and Noguchi (1995, 1997) take as evidence for the NP status of these elements. As mentioned by Elbourne (2005), however, what is overlooked here is the fact that these modifiers, when attached to *kare* or *kanosyo*, are obligatorily interpreted as non-restrictive modifiers. Thus, the most accurate translation of *tiisai kanozyo* would be 'she, who is short.' Given that non-restrictive modification (or

---

[9] Elbourne (2005) reports that judgments differ sharply among speakers as to the well-formedness of *dono-kare*. Presumably, for those speakers who find *dono-kare* grammatical, it is coerced into meaning 'which male person' in much the same way as in English sentences like *Is it a he or a she?*, as Elbourne suggests. Note that the well-formedness of *dono-hito* 'which person' is uncontroversial.

apposition) relations hold between two DPs, it follows that *kare* and *kanozyo* cannot be NPs.[10]

If overt third-person pronouns are not NPs, one might wonder why Japanese imposes more stringent restrictions on the repetition of personal pronouns than English. Recall (46), repeated here as (57).

(57) %Kare-wa kare-ga   kare-no   sigoto-o   si-tai   toki-ni
     he-TOP   he-NOM   he-GEN   work-ACC   do-want.to   when-PART
     kare-no   sigoto-o   suru.
     he-GEN   work-ACC   do
     'He does his work when he feels like doing it.'

As mentioned, to make the sentence sound natural, all but the first instance of *kare* need to be unexpressed.

(58) Kare-wa sigoto-o   si-tai   toki-ni   sigoto-o   suru.
     he-TOP   work-ACC   do-want.to   when-PART   work-ACC   do
     'He does his work when he feels like doing it.'

I speculate that this is due to an independent principle favoring a more attenuated anaphoric form over a less attenuated one where appropriate (i.e., a pragmatic/economy principle implemented in different ways by different authors (Levinson 1987, cf. Givón 1983; Ariel 1990, among others)). If this is right, the difference in acceptability between the Japanese sentence in (57) and its English counterpart is reduced to the fact that English does not have the option of using *pro*. Then the observed restriction on the repetition of pronouns does not necessarily buttress the argument that Japanese pronouns are syntactically NPs.

I have so far provided ample evidence against the NP analysis of overt third-person pronouns in Japanese, and have shown that it has serious empirical problems and lacks substantial supporting evidence. The question still remains, however, as to what *kare* and *kanozyo* actually are. Analyz-

---

[10] It should be noted that there are cases in which restrictive modification is possible with *kare* and *kanozyo*. In such cases, however, *kare* and *kanozyo* are interpreted as 'boyfriend' and 'girlfriend,' respectively (e.g., *watasi-no kare* 'my boyfriend'). Also, it seems that judgments differ among speakers as to whether *kare* and *kanozyo* can co-occur with (definite) demonstrative determiners. Indeed, Hinds (1971: 151) and Noguchi (1997: 777) report opposite judgments on this.

ing them as regular Condition B pronouns would bring us back to square one. So it is not a viable option. In what follows, we will consider the possibility that they are neither common nouns nor ordinary pronouns.

3.3.7. Japanese Third-Person Pronouns as Demonstratives (Kitagawa 1981; Hoji 1990, 1991)

Based on historical considerations, Kitagawa (1981) suggests that *kare* is pronominal in some respects while also being associated with a specific demonstrative/deictic function. To quote Kitagawa:

(59) A historically more accurate rendering of *kare* may be 'that one in question' rather than 'he.' Its present day use, although popularized in this day of global communication as a form that corresponds to English *he* (and its counterparts in other Germanic, Romance, and Slavic languages), seems to retain yet a strong demonstrative /deictic sense, with predilection for a specific reference.

(Kitagawa 1981: 71)

Under this approach, the peculiar binding-theoretic behavior of *kare* is attributed to its demonstrative/deictic character. In fact, there is a relatively broad consensus that Japanese third-person pronouns historically derive from deictic demonstrative expressions (Sansom 1928, among others).

Hoji (1990, 1991) brings this idea to the fore and attempts to derive the binding-theoretic properties of *kare* from its demonstrativity. The idea is that *kare* is a deictic demonstrative, which means that it can only refer.

In this connection, let us observe the paradigm of deictic demonstratives in Japanese. The *ko*-series, *so*-series, and *a*-series express different degrees of distance from the speaker. The following table, adapted from Martin (1975: 1066), is a list of deictic demonstratives in Japanese.

	proximal	mesial	distal
individual	kore "this thing"	sore "that thing"	are "that thing"
place	koko "this place"	soko "that place"	asoko "that place"
direction; alternative	kotira "this way"	sotira "that way"	atira "that way"
adnominal	kono "this"	sono "that"	ano "that"
adverbial (of manner)	koo "in this manner"	soo "in that manner"	aa "in that manner"

Table 3.2 Deictic Demonstratives in Japanese

The *ko*-series demonstratives indicate that the thing referred to is close to the speaker, while the *so*-series indicate proximity to the hearer. The *a*-series express that the entity in question is distant from both the speaker and the hearer. Hoji claims that *kare* and *kanozyo* fall into the category of the *a*-series (see Hoji 1991 for philological references).

However, as Hoji (1991: 288) himself is aware, this claim is undermined by the fact that *kare* does not belong to any paradigm despite the fact that true demonstratives systematically form a morphological paradigm, as we just witnessed.

(60) a. *ka(so)ko (intended as: a(so)ko 'that place')
    b. *katira (intended as: atira 'that way')
    c. *kaa (intended as: aa 'in that way')
    d. *kannani (intended as: annani 'that much')

(Hoji 1991: 288)

Furthermore, *kare* seems to be constrained differently than the *a*-series demonstratives in terms of coreference, as the following contrast shows (examples taken from Noguchi 1995: 29).

(61) a. John$_1$-wa kare$_1$-no titioya-ga kirai-da.
John-TOP he-GEN father-NOM dislike-COP
'John dislikes his father.'
b. #John$_1$-wa ano-hito$_1$-no titioya-ga kirai-da.
John-TOP that-person-GEN father-NOM dislike-COP
'John dislikes that person's father.'

It should also be pointed out here that being demonstrative does not necessarily entail being exclusively deictic. It is not uncommon for demonstratives to have non-deictic usages. Indeed, there are cases in which demonstratives function as bound variables, as Hoji himself reports. Following are some attested examples of demonstratives used as bound variables.

(62) Every logician$_1$ was walking with a boy near that logician$_1$'s house.

(Evans 1977: 491)

(63) Every boy$_1$ dates a girl who adores that boy$_1$.

(Noguchi 1997: 785)

(64) Mary talked to no senator$_1$ before that senator$_1$ was lobbied.

(Elbourne 2005)

In Japanese, it has been reported in the literature (Nishigauchi 1986; Hoji 1991; Ueyama 1998, among others) that the *so*-series demonstratives can receive bound-variable interpretations. In (65a) and (65b), *sono kaisya* 'that company' is bound by the quantificational subject *dono kaisya(-mo)* 'every company' (examples taken from Noguchi 1995:73).

(65) a. Dono kaisya$_1$-mo sono kaisya$_1$-ga itiban-da to
every company-PART that company-NOM best-COP COMP
omotteiru.
think
'Every company thinks that that company is the best.'
b. Dono kaisya$_1$-mo sono kaisya$_1$-no seihin-o
every company-PART that company-GEN product-ACC
homeru.
praise
'Every company praises that company's products.'

Thus, even if *kare* and *kanozyo* are genuine demonstratives, it does not necessarily follow that they cannot be bound. Since demonstrativity is neither a necessary nor a sufficient condition for unbindability, Hoji's (1990, 1991) analysis is vulnerable to criticism.

That said, this problem turns out to be only apparent once we take into account the recent observations made by Hoji et al. (2000) and Hara (2002). Contrary to the widely-held view that Japanese overt third-person pronouns cannot function as bound variables, these authors report that there are cases in which *kare* and *kanozyo* can be construed as bound variables under certain restricted environments. For example, *kare* can be bound by the quantificational subject in (66a) and (66b).

(66) a. ?Dono gakusei$_1$-mo sensyuu kare$_1$-o suisensita sensei-ni
every student-PART last.week he-ACC recommended teacher-DAT
orei-o okutta.
present-ACC sent
'Every student$_1$ sent a present to the teacher who recommended him$_1$ last week.'

(Hoji et al. 2000: 142)

b. [Dono nooberusyoo zyusyoo sakka]$_1$-mo kare$_1$-no
every Nobel.Prize winning author-PART he-GEN
hisyo-o turetekita.
secretary-ACC brought
'Every Nobel Prize winning author$_1$ brought his$_1$ secretary.'

(Hoji et al. 2000: 142)

The two sentences in (66) have the following interpretations, respectively.

(67) a. For every x, x a student, x sent a present to the teacher who recommended x last week.
b. For every x, x a Nobel Prize winning author, x brought x's secretary.

This means that the generalization stated in (16), repeated here as (68), is not accurate.

(68) Overt third-person pronouns in Japanese can only refer.

Hoji et al.'s and Hara's observations suggest that the question that needs to be asked is not why Japanese overt third-person pronouns cannot be bound but why Japanese third-person pronouns can receive bound-variable interpretations only in a subset of the contexts where bound pronouns in other languages (such as English) can occur. In what follows, we will take a closer look at the observations made by Hoji et al. (2000) and Hara (2002) and their analyses. Then I will present my own analysis.

3.4. The "Bindability" of Overt Third-Person Pronouns: Previous Studies

3.4.1. Hoji et al. (2000)

Hoji et al. (2000) present the data in (66), repeated here as (69), to show that it is not entirely impossible for *kare* to function as a bound variable.

(69) a. ?Dono gakusei$_1$-mo sensyuu kare$_1$-o suisensita sensei-ni
every student-PART last.week he-ACC recommended teacher-DAT
orei-o okutta.
present-ACC sent
'Every student$_1$ sent a present to the teacher who recommended him$_1$ last week.'
(Hoji et al. 2000: 142)

b. [Dono nooberusyoo zyusyoo sakka]$_1$-mo kare$_1$-no
every Nobel.Prize winning author-PART he-GEN
hisyo-o turetekita.
secretary-ACC brought
'Every Nobel Prize winning author$_1$ brought his$_1$ secretary.'
(Hoji et al. 2000: 142)

Building on Ueyama's (1998) theory, Hoji et al. (2000) attempt to answer the question of why binding of *kare* is highly restricted compared to binding of the English pronoun *he*.

According to Ueyama, individual-denoting NPs (or DPs) in natural language are classified into three categories.

(70) a. D-indexed NPs (e.g. John$_{D-3}$)
   b. 0-indexed NPs (e.g. he)
   c. I-indexed NPs (e.g. [that student]$_{I-5}$)

What makes D-indexed NPs distinct from 0- and I-indexed NPs is that the former, being referentially independent, do not require a linguistic antecedent whereas the latter do require a linguistic antecedent. D-indexed NPs are interpreted by being connected to an individual "that the speaker knows by his direct experience" (Ueyama 1998: 182). This connection, Hoji et al. (2000: 147) state, "is established independently of other NPs. From this it immediately follows that a D-indexed NP cannot be a bound variable".

Unlike D-indexed NPs, both 0-indexed NPs and I-index NPs can be interpreted as bound variables, but the mechanisms whereby they receive bound-variable readings are different. A 0-indexed NP is referentially defective so that it must enter into a Formal Dependency (FD) in order to be interpreted, whereas an I-indexed NP, whose classic example is an E-type pronoun, is "a free variable whose ultimate referent is determined by making reference to its co-I-indexed antecedent" (Hoji et al. 2000: 149). The latter forms an Indexical Dependency (ID) with a co-indexed NP antecedent.

Ueyama further argues that FD and ID are subject to distinct conditions. FD is subject to the following conditions.

(71) *Formal Dependency (FD)*
   a. Structural condition:
      *FD(α,β) if α does not c-command β at LF.
   b. Lexical condition:
      *FD(α,β) if β is a ^{large}NP.

A ^{large}NP (as opposed to ^{small}NP) refers to an informationally heavy NP. When β is interpreted as a pure bound variable, the semantic content of β will be ignored. Since a ^{large}NP carries too much semantic content to be ignored, it cannot qualify as β in FD(α,β) owing to the principle of recoverability. Hence the lexical condition on FD, given in (71b).

ID is subject to the following conditions.

(72) *Indexical Dependency (ID)*
   a. Structural condition:
      *ID(α,β) if α does not precede β at PF.

b. Lexical condition:
  *ID(α,β) if α is an A-type QP[11].

The condition in (72a) has the effect of blocking reconstruction. Thus, unlike 0-indexed NPs, I-indexed NPs fail to show reconstruction effects.

Based on Ueyama's classification, Hoji et al. (2000) argue that English third-person pronouns such as *he* can be used as any of the three types of NP.

(73)
D-index	I-index	0-index
he		

As such, *he* can be used as a referential pronoun, as an E-type pronoun, and as a pure bound variable.

Japanese third-person pronouns, on the other hand, can be used either as D- or I-indexed NPs but not as 0-indexed NPs.

(74)
D-index	I-index	0-index
kare		

This means that the bound-variable construal of *kare* obtains via ID but not via FD. It thus follows that third-person pronouns in Japanese can be interpreted as bound variables in a subset of the contexts in which bound third-person pronouns in English are licensed. Hoji et al. (2000) further report that there is a certain degree of inter-speaker variation with respect to whether *kare* can be 0-indexed. They argue that the unstable nature of Japanese third-person pronouns is due to the fact that these pronouns were coined only about a hundred years ago (for the purpose of translating foreign texts into Japanese), and as such their use has not been completely stabilized.

The claimed advantage of Hoji et al.'s (2000) analysis is that it captures the correlation between binding and reconstruction. As mentioned above, according to Ueyama's theory, I-indexed NPs (as opposed to 0-indexed NPs) do not undergo reconstruction. Then, it is expected that (for most speakers) *kare* does not show reconstruction effects. Indeed, fronting the indirect ob-

---

[11] Examples of A-type QPs include NP-*sae* 'even NP,' *kanarinokazu-no* NP 'most of the NPs,' *10 izyoo-no* NP 'ten or more NPs,' *55%-no* NP '55% of the NPs,' NP1 *to* NP2 (*to*) 'NP1 and NP2,' NP1 *ka* NP2 (*ka*) 'either NP1 or NP2.' See Ueyama (1998) for details.

ject together with the relative clause in (75) makes binding of *kare* impossible.

(75) ?Dono gakusei$_1$-mo sensyuu kare$_1$-o suisensita sensei-ni
every student-PART last.week he-ACC recommended teacher-DAT
orei-o okutta.
present-ACC sent
'Every student$_1$ sent a present to the teacher who recommended him$_1$ last week.'

(Hoji et al. 2000: 142)

(76) *[Sensyuu kare$_1$-o suisensita sensei-ni] dono gakusei$_1$-mo
last.week he-ACC recommended teacher-DAT every student-PART
t orei-o okutta.
present-ACC sent
'Every student$_1$ sent a present to the teacher who recommended him$_1$ last week.'

Hoji et al. (2000) also report that those speakers who allow *kare* to be interpreted as a pure bound variable (i.e., those who allow *kare* to be 0-indexed) also allow the covariant interpretation of *kare* to be reconstructed, as predicted by their analysis.

To sum up, Hoji et al.'s (2000) point is that there are three types of NP (or DP) that exhibit distinct binding and reconstruction patterns, as summarized below.

(77) a. NPs that can be bound (by any type of QP) and can show reconstruction effects.
  b. NPs that can be bound (by certain types of QP) and do not show reconstruction effects.
  c. NPs that cannot be bound at all.

These three categories bear different types of indices and follow distinct ways to form referential dependencies with their antecedents. The English pronoun *he* may be used as any of the three in (77), whereas *kare* can be used as (77b) or (77c) but not as (77a) (aside from some inter-speaker variation).

Hoji et al.'s (2000) observations are of considerable importance in that they bring to light the fact that the premise almost all previous studies were based on is actually false. As mentioned earlier, the true question that needs to be asked, therefore, is not why Japanese overt third-person pronouns cannot be bound but why Japanese third-person pronouns can receive bound-variable interpretations only in a subset of the contexts where bound pronouns in other languages (such as English) can occur.

Although Hoji et al. address the "right" question, the answer they offer does not seem sufficiently explanatory. As far as the binding properties of *kare* are concerned, their analysis is essentially a restatement of the observed facts rather than an explanation. Under their analysis, it is arbitrarily assumed that the pronoun *he* can be 0-indexed but *kare* cannot (for many speakers). The question thus remains as to why this should be the case. As such, Hoji et al.'s account does not offer a fundamental answer to the question of why binding of *kare* is not constrained in the same way as the English pronoun *he*.[12]

3.4.2. Hara (2002)

Let us next review Hara (2002), who extends Ariel's (1990) Accessibility Theory to the availability of bound-variable readings for *kare* and *kanozyo*. According to Accessibility Theory, the choice of referential forms is determined on the basis of the degree to which their referents are accessible to the addressee's memory.[13] Ariel claims that anaphoric expressions are accessibility markers in the sense that different anaphoric forms are used to mark different degrees of mental accessibility in order to guide addressees' retrievals of the intended referents.

There are several factors that play significant roles in determining the degree of accessibility. Some entities (e.g., speaker and addressee, sentence and discourse topics, etc.) are inherently more easily retrievable so that they have higher accessibility. Also, the degree of accessibility is affected by the

---

[12] This is not to say Hoji et al.'s analysis is wrong. In fact, their account and my proposal are not incompatible, and to that extent, it might be possible to integrate the two approaches.

[13] See also Tomlin (1987) and Tomlin and Pu (1991), who offer experimental evidence in support of the claim that the selection of referential forms is tied to cognitive processes of attention.

number of potential antecedents for a given anaphoric form in a given context; in a context where an anaphoric expression has more than one potential antecedent, it is less easy for the addressee to retrieve the intended referent. Thus, the more competing antecedents there are, the less accessible the intended antecedent is. Another factor that affects the degree of accessibility is the distance between an anaphoric expression and its intended antecedent. Hara (2002) argues that the notion of distance here should be defined in structural terms; that is, the more maximal projections there are between a given anaphoric form and its antecedent, the less accessible the antecedent is.

Different degrees of accessibility, Ariel argues, are marked by different linguistic forms in accordance with the following accessibility marking scale (Ariel 1994: 30).[14]

(78) *The Accessibility Marking Scale*
zero < reflexives < agreement markers < cliticized pronouns < unstressed pronouns < stressed pronouns < stressed pronouns + gesture < proximal demonstrative (+NP) < distal demonstrative (+NP) < proximal demonstrative (+NP) + modifier < distal demonstrative (+NP) + modifier < first name < last name < short definite description < long definite description < full name < full name + modifier

Zero anaphors (i.e., null pronouns) are the highest accessibility markers, and full names with modifiers are the lowest accessibility markers on the scale. The idea is that the higher the accessibility of a given referent, the higher the accessibility marker used to retrieve it. Hara (2002: 86) slightly modifies Ariel's accessibility marking scale, and proposes the following (partial) scale for Japanese anaphoric expressions.

(79) *Accessibility Marking Scale in Japanese*
zibun (self) < zero pronouns < third person pronouns < *sono* NP (*that* NP)

The highest on this scale is the anaphor *zibun*, followed by zero pronouns, third person pronouns and then *sono* NP "*that* NP". Let us consider how the contrast in grammaticality between (80a) and (80b) is explained under

---

[14] See Prince (1981) and Givón (1983) for similar ideas.

the accessibility-based account.

(80) a. Dono gakusei$_1$-mo {zibun$_1$-ga/ø$_1$} katu to omotteiru.
every student-PART self-NOM win COMP think
'Every student thinks that he will win.'
b. *Dono gakusei$_1$-mo kare$_1$-ga katu to omotteiru.
every student-PART he-NOM win COMP think
'Every student thinks that he will win.'

In (80a–b), the antecedent *dono gakusei-mo* 'every student' is close to the dependent term, and is therefore highly accessible. Thus, *zibun* or a null pronoun can be used as an appropriate anaphoric form that can take *dono gakusei-mo* as antecedent, whereas *kare*, being a low accessibility marker, is not a suitable anaphoric form here.[15] In other words, the antecedent is "too prominent for *kare* to be anaphoric to" (Hara 2002: 88). Hence the contrast.

Let us now consider the following example, where *kanozyo* can be construed as a variable bound by a quantificational expression.

(81) [Sono ondai-ni haitta] zyosi gakusei-no daremo$_1$-ga
that music.college-to entered female student-GEN everyone-NOM
[kanozyo$_1$-no sainoo-o mottomo yoku hikidasi-te kureru]
she-GEN talent-ACC most fully bring.out do.the.favor
sensei-ni dea-e-ta.
teacher-DAT meet-can-PAST
'Every one of the female students who entered that music college was able to meet a teacher who could bring out her talent to the full extent.'

(Hara 2002: 83)

In this case, although the dependent term is linearly adjacent to the antecedent QP, the two expressions are structurally sufficiently distant from each other so that the use of the low accessibility marker *kanozyo* is justified.

The point of Hara's analysis is that the degree of the bindability of a dependent term correlates with the degree of the accessibility of an antecedent. It is therefore not surprising that a null pronoun does not pattern with

---

[15] Hara (2002) discusses another factor that purportedly makes binding of third-person pronouns less available. See Hara (2002) for details.

kare in terms of binding because the former is a higher accessibility marker, whereas the latter is a lower accessibility marker.

While Hara's analysis offers a possible rationale for why binding of overt third-person pronouns in Japanese is constrained differently from binding of null pronouns in the same language, it does not offer any clear predictions as to the specific way the binding-theoretic properties of overt and null pronouns should or should not differ. It is not clear, for instance, how his analysis accounts for the fact that there are cases in which *kare/kanozyo* can be replaced with *zibun* or a null pronoun without affecting the availability of bound-variable readings. By way of illustration, the grammaticality of (81) remains intact even if *kanozyo* is replaced with *zibun* or a null pronoun.

(82) [Sono ondai-ni haitta] zyosi gakusei-no daremo$_1$-ga
that music.college-to entered female student-GEN everyone-NOM
[zibun$_1$-no/ϕ sainoo-o mottomo yoku hikidasi-te kureru]
self-GEN talent-ACC most fully bring.out do.the.favor
sensei-ni dea-e-ta.
teacher-DAT meet-can-PAST
'Every one of the female students who entered that music college was able to meet a teacher who could bring out her talent to the full extent.'

Still another problem is that there are cases in which increasing the structural distance between a third-person pronoun and its antecedent QP does not improve but rather detracts from the bindability of the pronoun. Consider the following sentences.

(83) ?Dono zyosi gakusei$_1$-ga kanozyo$_1$-no kimono-o minna-ni
which female student-NOM she-GEN kimono-ACC everyone-DAT
miseta no?
showed Q
'Which female student showed everyone her kimono?'

(84) *?Dono zyosi gakusei$_1$-ga [$_{CP}$ [$_{TP}$ kanozyo$_1$-no kimono-ga
which female student-NOM she-GEN kimono-NOM win
kirei-da] to] omotteiru no?
beautiful-COP COMP think Q
'Which female student thinks that her kimono is beautiful?'

In (83), *kanozyo* sits in the possessor position of the object in the matrix clause, whereas in (84), it is in the possessor position of the subject in the embedded clause. Thus, it is expected under Hara's account that (84) should be better than (83) because the former has a greater number of maximal projections intervening between *kanozyo* and its antecedent. (Recall that Hara claims that the more maximal projections there are between a given anaphoric form and its antecedent, the less accessible the antecedent is.) However, the reality is otherwise. Sentence (84) is, in fact, worse than (83), though admittedly the judgments are subtle.

It is most likely that memory and accessibility play an important role in anaphora resolution in discourse (a view with which I concur), but it is highly unlikely that the constraints on the binding of overt third-person pronouns in Japanese can be satisfactorily accounted for in terms of mental accessibility alone.

3.5. The Antilogophoricity Account

In what follows, I will propose that Japanese third-person pronouns should be characterized as epithets, and as such they can function as bound variables only when they satisfy both Condition B and the so-called antilogophoricity constraint.

3.5.1. Epithets and Antilogophoricity

Before we proceed, let us first look into the properties of epithets in English. Epithets are generally characterized as DPs (typically consisting of either a definite article or a demonstrative with an NP) that behave in much the same way as pronouns. Semantically, they have descriptive content and typically carry evaluative (often negative) connotations. Jackendoff (1972: 110) observes that epithets are pronoun-like in that they can take a non-local antecedent within the same sentence, as shown below.

(85) I wanted Charlie$_1$ to help me, but the bastard$_1$ wouldn't do it.

(86) Irving$_1$ was besieged by a horde of bills and the poor guy$_1$ couldn't pay them.

(87) Although the bum₁ tried to hit me, I can't really get too mad at Harry₁.

Moreover, Hornstein and Weinberg (1990) note that epithets can be construed as bound variables just like pronouns, as exemplified below (see also example (98)).

(88) John criticized every senator in private while praising the bastard in public.

(89) John will buy no wine before the damn thing is ready to drink.

In the sentences above, the epithets *the bastard* and *the damn thing* are bound by *every senator* and *no wine*, respectively. Thus, sentence (89), for instance, means much the same as 'No wine is such that John will buy it before it is ready to drink.' Hornstein and Weinberg argue that the quantificational DPs *every senator* and *no wine* undergo Quantifier Raising at LF, which makes A'-binding of the epithets possible. The LF representations of (88) and (89) are roughly illustrated as follows. (Irrelevant details are omitted.)

(90) [TP [QP every senator]₁ [TP John criticized [QP every senator] in private [while praising the bastard₁ in public]]]

(91) [TP [QP no wine]₁ [TP John will buy [QP no wine] [before the damn thing₁ is ready to drink]]]

Hornstein and Weinberg claim that given that variable binding requires a c-command relation between an operator and the variable that it binds, the availability of bound-variable interpretations for the epithets in these sentences suggests that they are A'-bound at LF. However, while the epithets in (88) and (89) are no doubt interpreted as bound variables, it is not evident whether they are actually bound from an operator position. This is because much evidence has been accumulated since Postal (1974) and Lasnik and Saito (1991) that suggests that accusative case is licensed in an A-position c-commanding into a VP adjunct. Consider the following sentence.

(92) The DA cross-examined none of the witnesses during any of the trials.

(Lasnik 2001: 104)

The example in (92) demonstrates that the NPI *any* in the adjunct phrase is licensed by the direct object *none of the witnesses*, indicating that the former is c-commanded by the latter. Lasnik and Saito (1991) also show that Condition C effects provide further evidence that accusative case is licensed in an A-position c-commanding into a VP adjunct. The contrast in grammaticality between (93a) and (93b) below is most naturally explained if we suppose that the accusative pronoun *him* in (93a) has moved to an A-position c-commanding *Bob* (thereby triggering a Condition C violation), whereas the nominative subject *he* in (93b) is licensed within the embedded clause.[16]

(93) a. ?*Joan believes him$_1$ [t$_1$ to be a genius] even more fervently than Bob$_1$'s mother does.
 b. Joan believes [he$_1$ is a genius] even more fervently than Bob$_1$'s mother does.

Given that an accusative-marked argument sits in an A-position c-commanding into an adjunct, the only conclusion that can be drawn from sentences (88) and (89) is that epithets can be bound by a quantificational antecedent. Crucially, the data do not necessarily warrant the conclusion that bound epithets must be A'-bound anaphora. The null hypothesis, then, is that epithets *can* be A-bound (as in the case of typical bound anaphora).[17]

The reason that Hornstein and Weinburg do not regard bound epithets as A-bound anaphora is that epithets are generally analyzed as R-expressions (Lasnik 1976, 1989, among others). The main argument for this view is based on the observation that epithets seem to exhibit Condition C effects. As exemplified below, it appears that they cannot occur in a position which is c-commanded by a co-valued argument in A-position (Lasnik 1976, 1989).

---

[16] As we will see in the next chapter, Condition C effects need to be treated with caution. That being said, the contrast here is telling.

[17] Since the issue of whether A'-binding of epithets is possible is orthogonal to the purposes of this book, I will not address it here. For epithets in resumptive contexts, see, among others, Aoun and Choueiri (2000), Aoun, Choueiri, and Hornstein (2001), and Safir (2004b: 63). Also, the jury is still out as to how sentences like *Every boy$_1$'s mother thinks that the bastard$_1$ is crazy* should be analyzed. See Kayne (1994: 23–24).

(94) a. *John₁ realizes that the sissy₁ is going to lose.
   b. *He₁ realizes that the sissy₁ is going to lose.
   c. *The sissy₁ realizes that the sissy₁ is going to lose.

(95) a. *John₁ thinks that I admire the idiot₁.
   b. *He₁ thinks that I admire the idiot₁.

If epithets are R-expressions, the ungrammaticality of these sentences straightforwardly follows because Condition C requires that R-expressions be A-free. What is interesting is that in languages like Thai, where R-expressions need not be (completely) free, epithets still cannot take a local antecedent, suggesting that they are subject to Condition B. On the basis of these observations, Lasnik (1989) proposes that epithets are "pronominal R-expressions", meaning that they concurrently act as pronouns and R-expressions. That is, they are subject to both Condition B and Condition C, which in turn means that epithets cannot be A-bound.

Narahara (1991) and Dubinsky and Hamilton (1998) independently argue, however, that the apparent Condition C effects are, in fact, attributed not to Condition C but to the antilogophoric properties of epithets (see also Pica 1994). These authors claim that the interpretation of epithets is constrained by Condition B and antilogophoricity restrictions.[18] Narahara's (1991) antilogophoricity constraint is based on Kuno's (1986: 62) disjointness condition on R-expressions, i.e., a condition that forces an R-expression in a logophoric complement to be disjoint in reference from logocentric NPs. Logophoric complements here refer to complement clauses embedded by predicates of speech, thought, psychological state and perception such as *say, think, believe, see, worry, bother claim*, and *belief.* (Narahara 1991: 71; Kuno 1987: 108) Logocentric NPs here refer to "the agent, source or experiencer argument of a logophoric verb" (Narahara 1991: 71).

Dubinsky and Hamilton (1998), on the other hand, claim that epithets are antilogophoric pronouns rather than R-expressions, and that they are subject to Condition B as well as the following antilogophoricity constraint.

---

[18] Given that coreference (as opposed to variable binding) is governed by Rule I rather than Binding Conditions (Grodzinsky and Reinhart 1993), it is more accurate to state that epithets are subject to (i) either Condition B or Rule I and (ii) the antilogophoricity constraint. For brevity's sake, Rule I is ignored here.

(96) *Antilogophoricity Constraint for Epithets*
An epithet must not be anteceded by an individual from whose perspective the attributive content of the epithet is evaluated.
(Dubinsky and Hamilton 1998: 689)

Let us take a look at the two proposals in more detail. Both accounts assume that epithets must conform to (some version of) Condition B, though Narahara maintains the idea that epithets are R-expressions. Under her approach, R-expressions are subject not to Condition C but to generalized Condition B, which requires that a non-anaphor (either a pronoun or an R-expression) must be free from a coargument of the same predicate. Dubinsky and Hamilton (1998), on the other hand, assume that epithets are pronouns, which is why they fall under Condition B. Both analyses correctly rule out sentences like the following.

(97) *John$_1$ admires the idiot$_1$.

It should be noted in this connection that epithets can function as dependent terms. For instance, they can function as a variable bound by a non-local antecedent when the antilogophoricity constraint is respected, as evidenced by the following example (recall also (88) and (89); see also Patel-Grosz 2012 for crosslinguistic data).

(98) Every stupid driver$_1$ ran over a man (who was) trying to give the idiot$_1$ directions.

This further supports the view that the structural disjointness condition relevant to epithets is not Condition C, which applies to referentially independent expressions, but rather is Condition B, which restricts the interpretation of (potentially) dependent expressions.

That said, since there is no a priori reason to assume that the antilogophoricity constraint does not apply in local contexts, let us assure ourselves that it is Condition B (and not antilogophoricity) that is responsible for the disjoint-reference effect in (97). The idea that epithets are subject to Condition B is supported by the fact that an epithet cannot take a local antecedent regardless of the type of the predicate it is an argument of.

(99) a. *John$_1$ admires the idiot$_1$.
 b. *John$_1$ hit the idiot$_1$.

c. *John₁ inadvertently exposed the idiot₁ while dancing.
d. *John₁ introduced the idiot₁ to the woman. (cf. I introduced John₁ to a woman who the idiot₁ had been dying to meet.)

Consider also the contrast between (100a–b). The antecedent *John* is the subject of *introduced* in both cases, but unlike (100a), the sentence in (100b), where the epithet *the son of a bitch* has a local antecedent, is ruled out.

(100) a. John₁ introduced Mary to the actress that [the son of a bitch]₁ used to hang out with.
b. *John₁ introduced [the son of a bitch]₁ to the actress that Mary used to hang out with.

These observations justify the claim that epithets are subject to Condition B.

Let us now turn to the proposed antilogophoricity restrictions. Dubinsky and Hamilton's definition of the antilogophoricity constraint predicts that sentences like (101) and (102) below are ruled out insofar as the epithets are read *de dicto*, but it incorrectly predicts that the same sentences are grammatical as long as the evaluation of the epithet is due exclusively to the current speaker's perspective (as opposed to the reported speaker's).

(101) *John₁ thinks that the fool₁ is going to lose.

(102) *Every student₁ thinks that the fool₁ is going to lose.

However, these sentences are unacceptable to many speakers with the given coindexation even if the ascription of foolishness to *John/every student* is due to the external speaker (i.e., the current speaker of the utterance), which suggests that the definition in (96) is too weak.[19] Note, though, that Dubinsky and Hamilton also state that an epithet must be disjoint in reference from SOURCE and SELF in Sells's (1987a) sense, which is essentially in

---

[19] For some speakers, sentences like *John₁ thinks that Mary believes that the fool₁ is going to lose* are better than (101) so long as the epithetic evaluation is due to Mary, which is actually compatible with Dubinsky and Hamilton's account. Since there is a fair amount of inter-speaker variation with respect to the acceptability of such sentences, I leave this issue for further research. See Aoun and Choueiri (2000) and Patel-Grosz (2012) for anti-locality effects.

line with Narahara's antilogophoricity constraint.[20] Since this definition does not suffer from the problem above, I assume that the relevant antilogophoricity constraint is such that it precludes epithets from being anteceded by SOURCE and SELF.

With this in mind, let us reconsider the sentences in (94) and (95). If the ungrammaticality of these sentences is due to antilogophoric effects rather than Condition C violations, then it is expected that epithets can take a (non-local) c-commanding antecedent, provided that their antecedent is not understood as the SOURCE or the SELF in the context. This expectation is borne out. Consider the following examples.

(103) John$_1$ ran over a man (who was) trying to give the idiot$_1$ directions.
(Dubinsky and Hamilton 1998: 688)

(104) Through an accumulation of slipups, John$_1$ (inadvertently) led his students to conclude that the idiot$_1$ couldn't teach.
(Dubinsky and Hamilton 1998: 688)

(105) My brother$_1$ invests in many projects that the idiot$_1$ thinks will make him rich.
(Haïk 1984: 204, fn21)

All the sentences in (103)–(105) are grammatical with the given coindexation even though the epithet is anteceded by a c-commanding argument. This is because in all these cases, the antecedent of the epithet is neither a SOURCE nor a SELF, thereby satisfying the antilogophoricity constraint. The grammaticality of these sentences is correctly predicted by the antilogophoricity accounts proposed by Narahara (1991) and Dubinsky and Hamilton (1998). At the same time, these observations cast doubt on the view that epithets are subject to Condition C; if they were, sentences (103)–(105) should be ruled out, contrary to fact.

To recap, English epithets are best analyzed as pronouns with antilogophoric properties, and as such they fall under Condition B and the antilogophoricity constraint, the latter of which prohibits epithets from being anaphoric to SOURCE and SELF antecedents.

---

[20] To be more precise, Dubinsky and Hamilton state that epithets must be disjoint in reference from SELF, which entails that they must also be disjoint from SOURCE.

3.5.2. Japanese Overt Third-Person Pronouns as Epithets

Let us now return to Japanese overt-third person pronouns. I will first argue that Japanese third-person pronouns such as *kare* and *kanozyo* are in fact epithets, claiming that they can function as bound variables just in case they satisfy both Condition B and the antilogophoricity constraint outlined above.

One might wonder, in the first place, whether, aside from their distributional properties, there is good reason to believe that Japanese third-person pronouns should be characterized as epithets. The answer is affirmative. As noted by Hinds (1975: 155), "there are a number of presuppositions, constraints, or prohibitions that prevent the free occurrence of *kare*". Among the restrictions on the use of *kare* is the prohibition against referring to social superiors. Hinds (1975) reports that the use of *kare* is avoided when referring to a social superior, especially if the speaker has some kind of relationship with the social superior (see also Noguchi 1995: 58, fn. 36; 1997: 778).[21] The oddity of the following sentence confirms his observation.

(106) #Kare-ga   o-mati-ni-nat-teiru.
       he-NOM   HON-wait-HON-HON-ASP
       'He is waiting.'

Here the verb *mati* 'wait' bears the honorific marking *o-X-ni-nar*, which implies that the speaker evaluates the referent of *kare* as socially superior to him/her, while the use of *kare* implies that the speaker does not evaluate its referent as socially superior to him/her. Thus the sentence in (106) sounds bizarre because of this contradiction. This squares nicely with the claim that Japanese third-person pronouns are epithets rather than garden-variety personal pronouns, considering that epithets generally carry evaluative connotations.[22]

---

[21] The use of the feminine form *kanozyo* is also avoided when referring to someone socially superior to the speaker. For other characteristics of Japanese third-person pronouns, see Hinds (1975, 1978).

[22] While the evaluative connotations of *kare/kanozyo* seem to be very subtle for some speakers (especially those in the younger generation), all the speakers I consulted confirmed, regardless of age, that they would avoid using *kare/kanozyo* to refer to their superiors. I take this to indicate that *kare* and *kanozyo* come with certain expressive content associated with the speaker's evaluation.

92   *Antilogophoricity and Binding Theory*

Another piece of support for the present account comes from Takubo's (1990) observation. In his study of crosslinguistic differences in the use of deictic/demonstrative expressions, Takubo (1990) notes an interesting restriction on the use of *kare*. Consider the following contrast between (107) and (108).

(107) A: I met Mr. Tanaka.
 B: a. Who is that?
   b. Who is he?

(108) A: Tanaka-san-ni   atta-yo.
   Tanaka-Mr.-DAT met-PART
   'I met Mr. Tanaka.'
 B: a. Sore-wa/Sono hito-wa   dare?
    that-TOP/that person-TOP who
    'Who is that/that person?'
   b. #Kare-wa dare?
    he-TOP who
    'Who is he?'

(adapted from Takubo 1990: 141)

In English, under contexts like (107), it is possible to felicitously ask about the identity of Mr. Tanaka by using either a demonstrative pronoun or a third-person pronoun. In Japanese, by contrast, it is not appropriate to use *kare* if the identity of the referent is not known to the utterer. This restriction is readily explained in the analysis proposed here. That is, in (108), B is not in a position to evaluate the person called Mr. Tanaka, and is therefore not in a position to use an epithet to refer to him. Thus, the infelicitousness of the use of *kare* in the context of (108) provides further support for the claim that Japanese third-person pronouns are characterized as epithets.

Having independently justified the treatment of Japanese third-person pronouns as epithets, we now look at how the present proposal captures the binding properties of Japanese overt third-person pronouns. Consider the following sentences.

(109) a. *Dono gakusei$_1$-mo   kare$_1$-o semeta.
    every student-PART he-ACC blamed
    'Every student blamed him.'

b. ?*Dono gakusei₁-mo kare₁-ga isya-ni naru to sinziteiru.
every student-PART he-NOM doctor-as become COMP believe
'Every student believes that he will become a doctor.'

Under the analysis proposed here, the unbindability of *kare* in the above sentences stems from different sources. In (109a), it is Condition B that makes it impossible for *kare* to be bound by the quantificational antecedent *dono gakusei(-mo)* 'every student'. In (109b), on the other hand, it is due to the antilogophoricity constraint that *kare* cannot be bound by *dono gakusei(-mo)*; that is to say, since *dono gakusei(-mo)*, being the subject of a world-creating verb (*sinziteiru* 'believe'), is the agent of the attitude report, it cannot be taken as antecedent of *kare*.

With this in mind, we are now in a position to reconsider the attested cases where overt third-person pronouns can be construed as bound variables. As we have seen, Hoji et al. (2000) and Hara (2002) are among the very few studies that recognize the availability of bound-variable interpretations for overt third-person pronouns in Japanese and address the question of why these pronouns can be bound only in certain restricted environments, though observations to the same effect were made even earlier. Below I list some representative instances reported in the literature where overt third-person pronouns can receive bound-variable readings.

(110) Dono nooberusyoo zyusyoo sakka₁-ga kare₁-no kuruma-de
which Nobel.Prize winning author-NOM he-GEN car-in
kita-no?
came-Q
'Which Nobel Prize winning author came in his car?'

(Hoji 1991: 298)

(111) ??Dono hito₁-ga kare₁-no saihu-o nakusita ka-ga
which person-NOM he-GEN wallet-ACC lost Q-NOM
mondai-ni natta.
issue-DAT became
'Which person lost his wallet became an issue.'

(Hoji 1991: 295)

(112) Mary-ga John-ni yorimo sakini Bill-ni kare-no
Mary-NOM John-DAT than earlier Bill-DAT he-GEN

hon-o suisens-ase-ta.
book-ACC recommend-CAUS-PAST
'Mary made Bill recommend his book earlier than (she made) John (recommend his book.)'

(Hoji 1997: 218)

(113) ?Dono gakusei$_1$-mo sensyuu kare$_1$-o suisensita sensei-ni
every student-PART last.week he-ACC recommended teacher-DAT
orei-o okutta.
present-ACC sent
'Every student sent a present to the teacher who recommended him last week.'

(Hoji et al. 2000: 142)

(114) [Sono ondai-ni haitta] zyosi gakusei-no daremo$_1$-ga
that music.college-to entered female student-GEN everyone-NOM
[kanozyo$_1$-no sainoo-o mottomo yoku hikidasi-te kureru]
she-GEN talent-ACC most fully bring.out do.the.favor
sensei-ni dea-e-ta.
teacher-DAT meet-can-PAST
'Every one of the female students who entered that music college was able to meet a teacher who could bring out her talent to the full extent.'

(Hara 2002: 83)

What has gone unnoticed in the literature is that the distribution of bound-variable occurrences of *kare/kanozyo* is markedly skewed to non-attitude contexts. In fact, none of these sentences involves indirect discourse, so that the antecedents of *kare/kanozyo* cannot be taken as the SOURCE (i.e., the one who makes the report) or as the SELF (i.e., the one whose mental state or attitude the content of the proposition describes). As a result, the antilogophoricity constraint is satisfied.[23] Because both Condition B and the antilogophoricity constraint are simultaneously satisfied, *kare* and *kanozyo* can be bound by a c-commanding antecedent.

---

[23] A few potential counterexamples are found in Hoji (1991: e.g., (31a, b)). Note also that Hoji acknowledges that there is variation among speakers with respect to the acceptability of those data.

If the analysis outlined here is on the right track, it is predicted that a sloppy reading (in addition to a strict reading) obtains if *kare* and *kanozyo* are placed in those contexts where Condition B and the relevant antilogophoricity constraint are respected. This prediction is, in fact, borne out.

(115) (Subeteno dansi gakusei nonakade) Taroo-dake-ga kare-no
 all male student among Taro-only-NOM he-GEN
 sainoo-o takaku hyookasuru sensei-ni deatta.
 talent-ACC highly admire teacher-DAT met
 '(Of all male students) only Taro met a teacher who thought highly of his talent.'

Ignoring any irrelevant readings where *kare* refers to someone other than Taro, the sentence in (115) has two possible interpretations. It entails either that the other male students did not meet a teacher who thought highly of Taro's talent, or that the other male students did not meet a teacher who thought highly of their talent. This is confirmed by the fact that the statement in (115) can be felicitously denied by uttering either (116a) or (116b).

(116) a. Iya, boku-mo Taroo-no sainoo-o takaku hyookasuru
 No I-also Taro-GEN talent-ACC highly admire
 sensei-ni deatta.
 teacher-DAT met
 'No, I also met a teacher who thought highly of Taro's talent.'
 b. Iya, boku-mo boku-no sainoo-o takaku hyookasuru sensei-ni
 No I-also I-GEN talent-ACC highly admire teacher-DAT
 deatta.
 met
 'No, I also met a teacher who thought highly of my talent.'

The possible entailments for (115) can be taken to indicate that Japanese overt third-person pronouns can not merely corefer but also serve as bound variables so long as Condition B and the antilogophoricity constraint are simultaneously satisfied. As expected, quantificational binding is likewise possible in the same context.

(117) Dono dansi gakusei₁-mo kare₁-no sainoo-o takaku hyookasuru
 any male student-PART he-NOM talent-ACC highly admire
 sensei-ni dea-e-nakat-ta.
 teacher-DAT meet-can-NEG-PAST
 'No male student could meet a teacher who thought highly of his talent.'

3.5.3. The Apparent Absence of Antilogophoric Effects

We have thus far seen that the distribution of bound pronouns in Japanese can be nicely captured if they are analyzed as epithets, i.e., antilogophoric pronouns. However, the present analysis as it stands seems to be too strong. For example, it fails to explain why sentences like the following do not display antilogophoric effects (see also examples (5a) and (5b)).

(118) a. Taroo₁-wa kare₁-ga katu to omotteiru.
 Taro-TOP he-NOM win COMP think
 'Taro thinks that he will win.'
 b. Taroo₁-wa Hanako-ga kare₁-o uttaeru to omotteiru.
 Taro-TOP Hanako-NOM he-ACC sue COMP think
 'Taro thinks that Hanako will sue him.'

In both of these sentences, *kare* refers to the person whose thought is being reported. Under the analysis presented here, this should be ruled out by the antilogophoricity constraint, contrary to fact.

 Recall also in this connection that a strict reading is readily available when an overt third-person pronoun is embedded in the complement clause of an attitude verb, as we saw in (8) repeated here as (119).

(119) (Subeteno dansi gakusei nonakade) Taroo-dake-ga Hanako-ga
 all male student among Taro-only-NOM Hanako-NOM
 kare-o uttaeru to omotteiru.
 he-ACC sue COMP think
 '(Of all male students) only Taro thinks Hanako will sue him.'

As mentioned earlier, the sentence in (119) entails that the other male students do not think that Hanako will sue Taro though it does not entail that the other male students do not think that they will be sued by Hanako. This suggests that even though *kare* cannot be bound by *Taroo*, coreference between them is still possible. However, the antilogophoricity constraint as it stands would incorrectly rule out this possibility. The question is, therefore, why only semantic binding (but not coreference) of Japanese overt third-pronouns seems to be subject to the antilogophoricity constraint. The contrast between the following two sentences illustrates this issue.

(120) a. Taroo$_1$-wa kare$_1$-ga daihyoo-ni erabareru to
Taro-TOP he-NOM representative-as be.selected COMP
omotteiru.
think
'Taro thinks that he will be selected as a representative.'
b. ?*Dono gakusei$_1$-mo kare$_1$-ga daihyoo-ni erabareru
every student-PART he-NOM representative-as be.selected
to omotteiru.
COMP think
'Every student believes that he will be selected as a representative.'

I argue that the apparent insensitivity of the referential use of *kare* and *kanozyo* to the antilogophoricity constraint is accounted for if we suppose that they can be realized not only as a full epithet phrase (as represented in (121a)) but also as an appositive epithet phrase that adjoins to a null pronoun (as represented in (121b)).

(121) a. [$_{DP}$ *kare/kanozyo* (= epithet phrase)]
b. [$_{DP}$ *pro* [$_{AppositiveP}$ *kare/kanozyo* (= epithet phrase)]]

This is reminiscent of Postal's (1972) idea that anaphoric epithets underlyingly consist of a pronoun and an appositive relative clause. What lies behind this idea is Jackendoff's observation (see (85)–(87)) that the distribution of anaphoric (or coreferential) epithets significantly overlaps with that of coreferential pronouns. Postal claims that Jackendoff's observation can be captured if we assume that epithets such as *the bastard* are derived from underlying structures like *he, who is a bastard*. While Postal's original analysis is not consonant with current theoretical assumptions, it is easy to recast it in terms of current syntactic theory by postulating a structure like (121b), where an appositive epithet phrase adjoins to a null pronominal anchor. Indeed, researchers like Patel-Grosz (2012) analyze English epithets as having such a structure (see also Collins and Postal 2012: Chapter 11; cf. Potts 2005). However, unless there is compelling evidence to the contrary, I assume that a covert pronominal structure like (121b) is possible in languages where *pro* is independently available.[24] This means that while Japanese epithet phrases are in principle structurally ambiguous between full DPs and appositive phrases with a null pronominal anchor, English epithet phrases are unambiguously full DPs unless they occur with an overt anchor.

An advantage of this analysis is that it can provide a straightforward explanation of why only variable binding seems to be subject to the antilogophoricity constraint. In the case of (121a), *kare* (or *kanozyo*) behaves the same way as English epithets; thus, it can be bound by or corefer with its antecedent so long as Condition B and the antilogophoricity constraint are simultaneously satisfied. On the other hand, if *kare* (or *kanozyo*) is composed of a null pronoun with an appositive modifier (= (121b)), it is constrained in the same way as ordinary null pronouns except that it cannot receive a bound-variable interpretation. The underlying idea here is that nonrestrictive modifiers can only be linked to referring expressions (Potts 2005 and references therein), which means that the host of an appositive cannot function as a bound variable. Thus, although *pro* can in principle be bound, binding of *pro* is disallowed under the configuration in (121b). To obtain a good idea of what is responsible for the contrast between (120a) and (120b), it is perhaps best to look at English (overt) analogues to the two sentences.

(122) a. John thinks that the bastard will be selected as a representative.

(*John = the bastard)

b. John thinks that he, the bastard, will be selected as a representative.

(^{ok} John = he)

(123) a. Every boy thinks that the bastard will be selected as a representative.

(*every boy = the bastard)

---

[24] Patel-Grosz (2012) takes the fact that epithets can be bound by a quantificational antecedent as evidence for postulating a null pronominal anchor. As we will see, however, this claim runs counter to the well-established observation that the host of an appositive phrase must be a referring expression. Cf. Potts (2005: 173ff.)

b. Every boy thinks that he, the bastard, will be selected as a representative.

(*every boy = he)

The Japanese sentence in (120a) can be assigned two distinct structures, one on a par with (122a) and the other with (122b). In (122a), *the bastard* cannot be anteceded by *John* due to the antilogophoricity constraint, whereas in (122b), *he* can be coreferential with *John*. In the latter case, the antilogophoricity constraint is irrelevant because *he* is not an antilogophoric pronoun. The reason that the presence of *the bastard* in (122b) does not run afoul of the antilogopohricity constraint is that a non-restrictive modifier is essentially an inserted comment by the speaker of the utterance (rather than the reported speaker), and as such it lies outside the purview of the logophoric center *John* in (122b). Given that appositive (non-restrictive) relatives behave as though they were coordinated root clauses (Ross 1967; Emonds 1979, among others), it is not surprising that the antilogophoric effect is circumvented here. The crucial point is, though, that whatever is responsible for the contrast between (122a, b) and (123a, b) is also responsible for the contrast between (120a) and (120b). Let us now consider (120b), which corresponds to (123a) and (123b). In (123a), *the bastard* cannot be anteceded by *every boy* due to the antilogophoricity constraint (just as in (122a) above). In (123b), since the pronoun *he* is the host for an appositive phrase, it can only be used as a referential pronoun. However, since *every boy* is a quantificational expression and thus lacks reference, coreference is not an option here. Therefore, there is no way that the pronoun *he* is anaphorically related to *every boy* in this sentence.

In sum, the structural ambiguity of *kare/kanozyo* gives the false impression that their referential use does not fall under the scope of the antilogophoricity constraint. The present analysis nicely captures the fact that if *kare* or *kanozyo* is anteceded by a logocentric subject, it must have a structure in (121b) and thus can only have a referential interpretation; hence the contrast in grammaticality between (120a) and (120b). Importantly, the anaphoric patterns we have seen justify the covert pronominal analysis of Japanese epithets, while at the same time casting doubt on the validity of the postulation of a covert pronominal structure for English epithets (à la Patel-Grosz (2012)).

Finally, given that epithet phrases can adjoin to a null pronoun, it is expected that antilogophoric effects are also not visible in the referential use of bona fide epithets in Japanese. This prediction is indeed borne out by the following examples.

(124) a. Taroo$_1$-wa yatu$_1$-ga katu to omotteiru.
Taro-TOP dude-NOM win COMP think
'Taro thinks that the dude will win.'
b. Taroo$_1$-wa yatu$_1$-o sizisita hito-o uragitta.
Taro-TOP dude-ACC support person-ACC betrayed
'Taro betrayed a person who supported the dude.'

In (124a), the antecedent of the epithet *yatu*—a derogatory term that roughly means 'dude'—is understood as the source of the embedded proposition, while in (124b), the antecedent is not understood as the SOURCE/SELF.[25, 26] Since the two sentences are equally fine, the antilogophoricity constraint seems, at first sight, not to be at work. As expected, however, *only*-modification reveals the hidden antilogophoric effects.

(125) a. Taroo-dake-ga yatu-ga katu to omotteiru.
Taro-only-NOM dude-NOM win COMP think
'Only Taro thinks that the dude will win.'
b. Taroo-dake-ga yatu-o sizisita hito-o uragitta.
Taro-only-NOM dude-ACC support person-ACC betrayed
'Only Taro betrayed a person who supported the dude.'

Ignoring any interpretations where *yatu* refers to an individual other than Taro, (125a) only allows a strict reading, while (125b) allows both strict and sloppy readings. (Under the sloppy interpretation of (125b), the sentence is false if, say, Jiro also betrayed a person who supported him (= Jiro).) The absence of a sloppy reading for (125a) is straightforwardly accounted for in the analysis presented here. That is, if the epithet *yatu* is syntactically real-

---

[25] Note that here the evaluation of the epithet is due to the external speaker's perspective (not Taro's).

[26] Here I intentionally avoid using those epithets that involve (incorporated) demonstratives (e.g., *aitu* 'that guy') because the anaphoric use of Japanese demonstratives is known to be subject to some idiosyncratic constraints. See, among others, Kuno (1973) for discussion on the anaphoric use of demonstratives.

ized as an epithet phrase alone (as in (121a)), it is interpreted as disjoint in reference from *Taroo* because of the antilogophoricity constraint. If it is realized as an appositive modifier attached to *pro* (as in (121b)), then the *pro* can corefer with *Taroo*, but cannot be interpreted as a bound variable because the host of an appositive must be a referring expression. Hence no sloppy reading is possible for (125a).

3.6. Summary of the Chapter and Remaining Issues

To sum up the discussion in this chapter, the most striking result of the present analysis is that it has uncovered the concealed antilogophoric properties of overt third-person pronouns in Japanese. I have proposed that Japanese third-person pronouns are in fact epithets, thereby functioning as bound variables only when they abide by both Condition B and the antilogophoricity constraint. I have also argued that the antilogophoric effects in the referential use of Japanese pronouns are masked by the fact that unlike English, Japanese allows a structure where a silent pronoun is juxtaposed with an appositive epithet phrase.

Note that the structural ambiguity account proposed here is not simply reducible to Noguchi's (1995, 1997) D/N distinction or Déchaine and Wiltschko's (2002) D/φ/N taxonomy. Recall that Noguchi (1995, 1997) and Déchaine and Wiltschko (2002) argue that the binding-theoretic properties of a pronoun are derived from its morphosyntactic makeup. Under Noguchi's approach, for example, pronouns are classified into D-pronouns (i.e., pronouns that belong to the category of D) and N-pronouns (i.e., pronouns that are morphosyntactically equivalent to nouns), only the former of which can function as bound variables. If we attempt to explain the binding properties of *kare/kanozyo* along the lines of Noguchi's approach, it must be concluded that so-called third-person pronouns in Japanese are ambiguous between D- and N-pronouns. But this leaves us with the question of why they behave as D-pronouns only in certain restricted contexts. Thus, the present analysis fares better in that it provides a principled account of when and why these pronouns can be interpreted as bound variables.

It should be emphasized that the proposed conditions on the binding of *kare/kanozyo* are presumably necessary rather than sufficient conditions; for there seem to be some other restrictions that constrain the bound-variable use of these pronouns. For one, Hoji (1991) reports that the more restricted the range of the variable bound by a *wh*-phrase is, the more readily *kare* can be bound by the *wh*-phrase, as demonstrated by the following set of sentences (examples (126b–d) taken from Hoji 1991: 297–98).

(126) a. *Ittai dare$_1$-ga kare$_1$-no kuruma-de kita no?
 on.earth who-NOM he-GEN car-in came Q
 'Who on earth came in his car?'

b. ??Dono hito$_1$-ga kare$_1$-no kuruma-de kita no?
 which person-NOM he-GEN car-in came Q
 'Which person came in his car?'

c. ?Dono sakka$_1$-ga kare$_1$-no kuruma-de kita no?
 which writer-NOM he-GEN car-in came Q
 'Which writer came in his car?'

d. Dono nooberusyo zyushoo sakka$_1$-ga kare$_1$-no kuruma-de
 which Nobel.Prize winning author-NOM he-GEN car-in
 kita no?
 came Q
 'Which Nobel Prize winning author came in his car?'

Likewise, it seems that quantificational expressions like *daremo* 'everyone' cannot bind *kare/kanozyo* unless the domain of quantification is explicitly restricted (cf. Hara 2002). Thus, straightforward sentences like (127a–b) below are unacceptable for many speakers. (Compare (127b) with (81).)

(127) a. ?*Daremo$_1$-ga kare$_1$-no hahaoya-o aisiteiru.
 everyone-NOM he-GEN mother-ACC love
 'Everyone loves his mother.'

b. ?*Daremo$_1$-ga [kanozyo$_1$-no sainoo-o mottomo yoku
 everyone-NOM she-GEN talent-ACC most fully
 hikidasi-te kureru] sensei-ni dea-e-ta.
 bring.out do.the.favor teacher-DAT meet-can-PAST
 'Everyone was able to meet a teacher who could bring out her talent to the full extent.'

These facts, of course, raise the following questions: What exactly qualifies as an antecedent of *kare/kanozyo*, and why? It might be noteworthy that the domain of quantification must be restricted to (contextually relevant) male individuals in the case of *kare* and to female individuals in the case of *kanozyo*. Then the observed restrictions might be due to the presuppositions of *daremo* and *kare/kanozyo*. Having said that, I leave these issues for future research. (See Hara 2002 for an accessibility-based account.)

Another property of Japanese third-person pronouns that remains to be accounted for is Lasnik's (1989: 161) observation that the reflexive *zibun* cannot bind them, as discussed in Section 3.3.2.

(128) John$_1$-ga   [kare$_1$-ga [zibun$_1$-ga tensai da   to] omotteiru to]
       John-NOM   he-NOM   self-NOM   genius COP   that think   COMP
       itta.
       said
       (Lit.) 'John said that he thinks that self is a genius.'

(129) *John$_1$-ga   [zibun$_1$-ga [kare$_1$-ga tensai da   to] omotteiru to]
       John-NOM   self-NOM   he-NOM   genius COP   that think   COMP
       itta.
       said
       (Lit.) 'John said that self thinks that he is a genius.'

Lasnik attributes the contrast between (128) and (129) to the general prohibition against the binding of a more referential expression by a less referential expression.

Closer scrutiny suggests, however, that the observed restriction is not a matter of structural binding. In fact, *zibun* generally cannot precede *kare* when they share the same antecedent.

(130) John$_1$-wa   [kare$_1$-no yuuzin to   zibun$_1$-ga itiban da   to]
       John-TOP   he-GEN   friend CONJ   self-NOM   best   COP   that
       omotteiru.
       think
       (Lit.) 'John thinks that his friend and self are the best.'

(131) ?*John$_1$-wa [zibun$_1$-no yuuzin to   kare$_1$-ga itiban da   to]
John-TOP self-GEN friend CONJ he-NOM best COP that
omotteiru.
think
(Lit.) 'John thinks that self's friend and he are the best.'

Under the present account, it is tempting to derive this co-occurrence restriction from the ban on conflicting empathy foci, which prohibits a sentence from containing logical conflicts in empathy relationships (Kuno 1987: 207, 2004: 316).[27] To be more specific, it has been claimed that the referent of *zibun* needs to be the target of the speaker's empathy (Kuno 1987: 254), while the referent of an epithet normally cannot be the target of the speaker's empathy (Corazza 2013). It has also been argued that word order is closely related to empathy (Kuno 1987: 232, 2004: 323). Then the observed co-occurrence restriction might possibly stem from some kind of empathy-related constraint. Certainly, further investigation is required to fully understand this phenomenon.

To conclude this chapter, it is now evident that many of the previous studies were, in part, on the wrong track in seeking properties that render Japanese third-person pronouns exclusively referential. We have seen that once confounding factors are appropriately controlled for, it becomes evident that antilogophoiricy plays a crucial role in determining the distribution and interpretation of *kare* and *kanozyo*. The findings reported here underscore the fact that the study of anaphora requires careful consideration of various factors that may conspire to obscure the true nature of the phenomenon under investigation.

---

[27] I thank Dominique Sportiche (p.c.) and Yuhi Inoue (p.c.) for suggesting this analytical possibility to me.

Chapter 4

Antilogophoricity and the Scope of Condition C

4.1. Condition C and Antilogophoricity

In generative grammar, names, (definite) descriptions, and epithets have often been classified together under the same rubric; they are called R-expressions, and are assumed to be subject to the same binding condition—Condition C of the Binding Theory. There are several versions of Condition C that have been proposed in the literature, but the following is commonly accepted as descriptively adequate.

(1) *Condition C*
 An R-expression must be pronoun-free.

The term "free" is used here in a technical sense, which is to say, the condition comes into play just in case an R-expression and a coreferential pronoun stand in a particular geometric relation in the syntax;[1] namely, an R-expression must not be coreferential with a pronoun that c-commands

---

[1] This is not to say that Condition C is computed within narrow syntax. Note also that even if Condition C is subsumed under Rule I (Grodzinsky and Reinhart 1993; Reinhart 2006; Reinhart 1983), c-command is still relevant because Rule I only applies in a configuration where variable binding is in principle possible.

it.[2] Since the disjoint-reference effects in Condition C configurations are empirically well-attested across languages, Condition C has been widely used as a diagnostic for probing syntactic structures.

Let us here pause and reflect on the lesson learned in the previous chapter. Recall that Dubinsky and Hamilton (1998) convincingly argued that English epithets should be characterized as antilogophoric pronouns, challenging the commonly-held view that they are R-expressions (cf. Narahara 1991). The reason that epithets were, until then, generally regarded as R-expressions was that the antilogophoric effects of epithets were *wrongly* diagnosed as Condition C effects.

Now that we are aware of this pitfall, Condition C is ripe for critical reexamination; it is worthwhile to scrupulously inspect other prima facie cases that have been identified as Condition C violations, and verify whether their putative ungrammaticality actually stems from Condition C. This is in fact not a trivial matter, considering, in particular, that it has been noted (or hinted) by some researchers (Kuno 1972, 1986, 1987, 2004; Sells 1987b; Narahara 1991; Dubinsky and Hamilton 1998) that non-epithet R-expressions likewise have antilogophoric properties, as exemplified below.[3] (Example (2a) is taken from Lakoff (1968: 55), (2b) from Kuno (1972: 162), (2c) from Kuno (1987: 105) and (2d–e) from van Hoek (1995: 312).)

(2) a. *The knowledge that John$_1$ had cancer bothered him$_1$.
   b. *That John$_1$ will be elected is expected by him$_1$.
   c. ??That Ali$_1$ was the best boxer in the world was claimed by him$_1$ repeatedly.
   d. *His$_1$ fear is that John$_1$ might have cancer.
   e. *Her$_1$ wish is that Sally$_1$'s daughter will become a physicist.

Let us start by assessing whether the deviance of these examples stems not from Condition C but from antilogophoricity restrictions. Consider first (2a). In this sentence, the relevant pronoun fails to c-command the R-expression that it is intended to corefer with. Moreover, the acceptability

---

[2] See Bruening (2014) for a recent proposal that the relevant syntactic relation is not c-command but what is called *phase-command*.

[3] For some speakers, some of these examples are not utterly unacceptable. This is not surprising in view of the fact that violations of discourse constraints often elicit less pronounced effects on acceptability than violations of grammatical conditions.

of the sentence fluctuates depending on the choice of the head noun in the subject. For example, replacing the head noun *knowledge* with *rumor* enhances the acceptability of the sentence even though the basic structure is kept intact.

(3) The rumor that John$_1$ had cancer bothered him$_1$.

The difference in acceptability between (2a) and (3) is straightforwardly accounted for if we suppose that R-expressions are antilogophoric; that is, they must be disjoint in reference from the logophoric center. In (3), John is not the author of the rumor, which means that the "the rumor that" clause in this sentence is not reporting on John's internal feeling. By contrast, the most natural interpretation of (2a) is that the "knowledge" is ascribed to John. Thus, the sentence violates antilogophoricity restrictions because *John* is not disjoint from the individual whose mental state the content of the proposition describes.[4]

One might nevertheless argue, along the lines suggested by Chomsky (1986: 167–168), that (2a) involves a structure analogous to (4) below.

(4) *[PRO$_1$ knowing that John$_1$ had cancer] bothered him$_1$.

On this view, (2a) contains a silent pronoun that acts as the subject of *knowledge*. If the PRO and *John* are interpreted as having the same referent, a Condition C violation ensues because *John* is no longer free from a c-commanding pronoun. That said, there seems no independent justification anywhere else that we need to postulate a PRO in (2a), and to that extent, the Condition C analysis of this sentence, though not implausible, is vulnerable to criticism (see Williams 1985).

Let us next look into (2b) and (2c). In neither of these cases does the pronoun seem to c-command the R-expression it corefers with. However, one might still argue that these cases are also ruled out by Condition C by assuming that the sentential subject undergoes LF reconstruction and that the pronoun is actually in a specifier position rather than forming a constituent with *by* (see Collins 2005). On this view, *John* in (2b) and *Ali* in (2c) are respectively c-commanded by a coindexed pronoun at LF, thereby violating

---

[4] As predicted, the sentence becomes acceptable if it is some unattributed general knowledge that is under discussion.

Condition C, as schematically represented below.

(5) [... [... [by [him₁ [... [that John₁ will be elected]]]]]]

(6) [... [... [by [him₁ [... [that Ali₁ was the best boxer in the world]]]]]]

However, this argument does not go through. First, it has been observed that A-movement generally bleeds Condition C, as demonstrated by the following contrast.[5]

(7) *It seems to him₁ that the claim that John₁ was asleep is correct.

(8) The claim that John₁ was asleep seems to him₁ to be correct.

(Chomsky 1993: 37)

This indicates that a reconstruction analysis of (2b) and (2c) seems to lack strong empirical support.

Second, the choice of the matrix verb affects the acceptability of these sentences. For instance, the following sentence is significantly better than (2c).

(9) That Ali₁ was the best boxer in the world was proven by him₁ repeatedly.

This fact comports well with the antilogophoricity account. That is, unlike in (2c), *him* in (9) is not construed as an intentional agent of the report, which means that it is not understood as the logophoric center. Hence comes the ameliorating effect.

Finally, let us scrutinize (2d) and (2e). Like the cases we have considered above, these sentences presumably fail to meet the structural description for Condition C. However, it is not a quixotic idea to claim that the possessors *his* and *her* c-command *John* and *Sally*, respectively. Prima facie support for such an analysis comes from the fact that sentences like those below allow for variable binding.

(10) Everyone₁'s mother thinks he₁'s a genius.

(Reinhart 1983: 177)

---

[5] Note that the name *John* resides in the complement clause of the noun *claim*, so that one cannot resort to a late adjunction analysis à la Lebeaux (1988).

(11) Nobody₁'s students should respect him₁.

(Reinhart 1983: 177)

Given that variable binding requires c-command, the above data suggests that a possessor argument c-commands out of the possessive DP that it is a specifier of (see Kayne 1994). However, the well-formedness of the following sentence poses a problem for such an approach.⁶

(12) His₁ fear led me to believe that John₁ might have cancer.

Under the antilogophoricity account, the contrast between (2d) and (12) is predicted. In the former, the *that*-clause expresses the content of John's fear whereas in the latter, the *that*-clause expresses the speaker's belief. The latter case is not ruled out because the embedded proposition is not narrated from John's perspective.

All in all, it is reasonable to assume that some kind of antilogophoricity restriction for R-expressions is necessary, independently of Condition C.

Let us turn to Condition C. It is important to ask, first, whether Condition C has its own raison d'être, because it might turn out that Condition C is subsumed under antilogophoricity restrictions.

There is good reason to believe that Condition C is needed independently of antilogophoricity restrictions; that is, disjoint-reference effects do arise in those Condition C environments where antilogophoricity restrictions are plainly not applicable. Consider the following examples.

(13) a. *It₁ is more famous than the designer of Royce Hall₁.
     b. Royce Hall₁ is more famous than its₁ designer.
     c. Its₁ designer is more famous than Royce Hall₁.

(14) a. *In 2002, they relocated it₁ to Myers Inc.₁'s current location
     b. In 2002, they relocated Myers Inc.₁ to its₁ current location.

(15) a. *It₁ was closed because a snow storm hit UCLA₁.
     b. Its₁ library was closed because a snow storm hit UCLA₁.

The pronouns in these examples refer to inanimate objects, which, metaphor-

---

⁶ Admittedly, this is not a strong piece of evidence against the Condition C analysis of (2d–e) because (2d–e) and (12) may have fundamentally different structures. See Schlenker (2003).

ical cases aside, cannot be taken as logophoric centers. Thus, the illicitness of the a-sentences in (13)–(15) cannot be chalked up to antilogophoric effects. Notice that disjoint-reference effects emerge just in case a pronoun c-commands an R-expression that it is anaphoric to. This suggests that, aside from the question of how it is implemented, Condition C is needed independently of antilogophoricity restrictions, and that the former is not simply reducible to the latter.

Considering that Condition C and antilogophoricity restrictions are independently motivated and coexist, it is an interesting thought experiment to ask what makes sentences like the following illicit.

(16) *He_1 knows that $John_1$ has cancer.

There are at least three logical possibilities: sentences like (16) are ruled out by (i) Condition C alone; (ii) the relevant antilogophoricity constraint alone; (iii) both Condition C and the relevant antilogophorictiy constraint. At first sight, the safest bet seems to be that (16) is in violation of both conditions because the offending pronoun c-commands the R-expression *John*, while at the same time its referent is the center of consciousness. Contrary to this expectation, however, I will suggest that the illicitness of sentences like (16) is in all likelihood due not to Condition C but to the antilogophoricity constraint alone.

I will further argue that cases like the following are ruled out not by Condition C but by antilogophoricity restrictions.

(17) *He_1 talked to Melba just before the police arrested $Joseph_1$.

(Safir 2004b: 79)

Notice that in this case, replacing the name *Joseph* with an epithet results in a grammatical sentence.

(18) He_1 talked to Melba just before the police arrested the poor $bastard_1$.

(Safir 2004b: 79)

The grammaticality of (18) is not surprising, given that epithets are antilogophoric pronouns subject to antilogophoricity restrictions as well as Condition B. Since the epithet *the poor bastard* is free in its local domain, and since the referent of *he* is (presumably) not a perspective holder (because

(18) does not involve indirect discourse), it is expected that the coindexation given in (18) is licit, and in fact it is. One might conclude from the contrast between (17) and (18) that (17) is ruled out by Condition C because the grammaticality of (18) seems to indicate that antilogophoricity requirements are satisfied.

Plausible though it may seem, this reasoning is not foolproof as it rests on a potentially mistaken assumption—namely, that antilogophoric effects occur in a uniform way. This may not be an innocuous assumption in view of the fact that a growing body of research suggests that logophoricity is not a uniform phenomenon but comes in different, albeit similar, varieties.

It is an unquestionable fact that logophoric phenomena are real, as testified by the very existence of logophoric pronouns, but, as Sells (1987a: 477) correctly points out, "there is no unified notion of logophoricity in the way that (presumably) there is for other features proposed to be relevant for anaphora, such as the presence of a subject".

That logophoricity defies a unified description is *ipso facto* an indication that it is not a primitive but is merely a cover term for a family of related phenomena. Indeed, this view is defended by Sells (1987a), and as we witnessed in Chapter 2, logophoric effects in fact come in varying patterns. Given this fact, there is no compelling reason a priori to assume that antilogophoricity is a primitive notion or a single homogeneous phenomenon. The new picture that emerges is, then, that just as logophoricity comes in different varieties, so too does antilogophoricity.

With all this in mind, the central thesis to be explored in this chapter is that names in English are "maximally" antilogophoric in the sense that they must be disjoint from all potential logocentric antecedents (SOURCE, SELF, and PIVOT), whereas epithets are not as antilogophoric as names in the sense that they must be disjoint from a subset of logocentric antecedents (SOURCE and SELF). To the extent that this hypothesis is tenable, the difference between (17) and (18) is not a telling piece of evidence that (17) must be a Condition C violation. Indeed, similar proposals have been made by Sells (1987b) and Dubinsky and Hamilton (1998), although I adopt a rather different angle to verify the hypothesis, as will be shown shortly.

I will then go on to examine the scope of Condition C, by taking a close look at those cases where both Condition C and the antilogophoricity constraint are in principle applicable. I will suggest the possibility that surprisingly many cases of what we call Condition C effects are, in fact, spurious; they are not attributed to Condition C but to antilogophoricity restrictions. The results of our investigation have significant consequences for the Binding Theory. That is, although Condition C and antilogophoricity restrictions are presumably independent conditions regulating coreference, they do not operate independently of each other. Rather, there is a division of labor between Condition C and antilogophoricity restrictions.

Two caveats are in order before we proceed. First, throughout, I restrict my attention to names in English and ignore other types of R-expressions. Second, I am only concerned with intended (or presupposed) coreference. It has been known for quite some time that Condition C effects consistently fail to arise in unknown (unestablished) or mistaken identity cases.

(19) (I think they gave my paper to Zelda Jones for review.) She praises Zelda to high heavens (and totally ignores my stuff.)

(Büring 2005: 153)

Sentence (19) is fine even if *she*, the reviewer, is in fact *Zelda Jones*. In this case, the identity of Zelda Jones and the reviewer has not been established among the discourse participants in the context, which has the effect of suspending Condition C. See Higginbotham (1985), Safir (2004a: 28), Büring (2005: 151ff.) for relevant discussion (see also Heim (1998) for discussion of "guises" and Schlenker (2005) for other exceptions to Condition C).

4.2. Names as Maximal Antilogophors

In Chapter 2, we observed patterns of logophoricity across languages. To recapitulate the point, logophoricity is characterized along two dimensions: (i) logophoric domains and (ii) logocentric antecedents. Although languages superficially exhibit a bewildering variety of logophoric domains and logocentric antecedents, there are certain implicational universals with respect to the way the range of possible logophoric domains and that of possible logocentric antecedents are restricted.

Of particular relevance to our investigation is Sells's (1987a) taxonomy of discourse roles. Recall that logocentric antecedents are classified into the following three types.

(20) a. SOURCE: the one who makes the report; the intentional agent of the communication
   b. SELF: the one whose mental state or attitude the content of the proposition describes
   c. PIVOT: the one from whose point of view the report is made; the one with respect to whose (space-time) location the content of the proposition is evaluated

According to Sells, languages differ with respect to which role qualifies as an antecedent of a logophoric expression. What is important here is that being a SOURCE entails being also a SELF as well as a PIVOT, and being a SELF entails being also a PIVOT. Thus, the fact that Japanese allows binding of *zibun* by a PIVOT predicts that it also allows *zibun*-binding by a SOURCE or a SELF. This is in fact the case.

(21) Taroo$_1$-wa [Yosiko-ga zibun$_1$-o aisiteiru to] itta.
   Taro-TOP Yoshiko-NOM self-ACC love COMP said
   'Taro$_1$ said that Yoshiko loved him$_1$.'

   (Sells 1987a: 461)

(22) [Yosiko-ga zibun$_1$-o musisita koto]-ga Taroo$_1$-o
   Yoshiko-NOM self-ACC ignored COMP-NOM Taro-ACC
   yuuutunisita.
   distressed
   'That Yoshiko ignored him$_1$ distressed Taro$_1$.'

   (Sells 1987a: 461)

(23) Takasi$_1$-wa [Yosiko-ga zibun$_1$-o tazunete-kita node]
   Takashi-TOP Yoshiko-NOM self-ACC visit-came because
   kanasigar-anakat-ta.
   become.sad-NEG-PAST
   'Takashi$_1$ was not sad because Yoshiko came to visit him$_1$.'

   (Sells 1987a: 472)

The sentences in (21), (22) and (23) demonstrate that *zibun* can be bound by SOURCE, SELF, or PIVOT antecedents.

114 *Antilogophoricity and Binding Theory*

With this much in place, let us now explore the hypothesis that names are maximally antilogophoric; namely, that they must be disjoint from all potential logocentric antecedents. The logic of this hypothesis is based on the observation that there is independent evidence that R-expressions resist coreference with a PIVOT. Bolinger (1979: 302) reports that (24a) is degraded compared to (24b).[7]

(24) a. ?/??I answered him₁ as soon as John₁ spoke.
 b. I recognized him₁ as soon as John₁ spoke.

Sells (1987b) suggests that the contrast is due to the fact that in (24a), John (= him) can possibly be interpreted as the PIVOT (presumably because the action of answering may imply some kind of communication to him), whereas in (24b) John (= him) cannot be so interpreted because "one cannot recognize someone whose point of view one is already taking" (p. 19). Sells further points out that a similar contrast is observed in the following pair.

(25) a. I got nothing from him₁ before John₁ left.
 b. ??I gave nothing to him₁ before John₁ left.

(Sells 1987b: 19)

He speculates that the deviance of sentence (25b) is tied to the fact that John (= him) is the target of empathy (and hence is the PIVOT) in the sentence.

Given that being a SOURCE or a SELF entails being also a PIVOT, and given that names resist coreference with a PIVOT, it follows that names should also resist coreference with a SOURCE and a SELF. Therefore, it is expected that names must be disjoint from all potential logophoric centers.

The idea put forward here is not new. Sells (1987b), inspired by Kuno (1972), proposes the following constraint, which is essentially in line with the hypothesis being explored here.

(26) Any reference to an individual bearing a discourse role must be syntactically expressed by a pronominal.

(Sells 1987b: 14)

---

[7] In Sells (1987b), the status of (24a) is reported as "??", while Bolinger's original judgment on the same sentence is "?". Hence I report it as "?/??" to do justice to their judgments.

What this means is that only pronominal forms may (though need not) be anaphoric to an individual that a discourse role is predicated of. In the case of a logophoric pronoun, association between the pronoun and a role-bearing individual is obligatory, while an ordinary pronoun may or may not be associated with a role-bearing individual.

Dubinsky and Hamilton (1998) restate (26) as a condition that prohibits R-expressions from bearing discourse roles. However, this is a potentially misleading statement because, if taken at face value, it would incorrectly predict that straightforward cases such as *Bill says that he is innocent* and *According to John, Bill was in Italy* should be ruled out.[8]

It is also important to note that the antilogophoricity constraint for R-expressions should not be interpreted as a requirement that R-expressions be disjoint from any DPs that bear discourse roles. For example, the following sentence is perfectly fine although *John* and *he* bear the SOURCE roles and refer to the same person.

(27) John$_1$ thought that he$_1$ said that I would win.

What is important here is that *John* does not lie within the logophoric domain relative to which *he* is the SOURCE, which means that *he* cannot be construed as a logophoric center for *John*. This contrasts with (28), where *John* is within the purview of the logophoric domain with respect to which *he* is the SOURCE.

(28) *He$_1$ thought that John$_1$ said that I would win.

The sentence in (28), therefore, runs afoul of antilogophoricity restrictions.

If this analysis is on the right track, Condition C effects need to be handled with caution. As suggested at the outset of this chapter, it is no longer self-evident whether sentences like the following are actually ruled out by Condition C, given that the referent of the pronoun is understood as the PIVOT.

(29) *He$_1$ talked to Melba just before the police arrested Joseph$_1$.

(Safir 2004b: 79)

---

[8] In fact, Sells (1987b: 5) explicitly states that the proposed constraint does not mean that roles may not be initiated by non-pronouns.

A few remarks on the notion of PIVOT are in order here. The idea underlying Sells's approach is that logophoricity is not a simple phenomenon but a cluster of related phenomena, and the common thread uniting these phenomena is the notion of "point of view" or "perspective".

It should be noted that while it is generally agreed that logophoric phenomena are closely related to point of view, there have been widely divergent views on this notion and its relevance to logophoricity (see Oshima 2006). Reinhart and Reuland (1993: 673, fn. 17) warn that "the attempt to reduce all actual occurrences of logophors to the same point-of-view mechanism, as in Sells 1987, renders the concept "point of view" rather vacuous". In particular, they state that the notion of PIVOT "has nothing to do with any familiar tests for point of view orientation" (*ibid.*) (see also Reinhart and Reuland 1991: 316).

Indeed, Sells's idea of PIVOT is rather vague. Sells (1987a: 456, fn. 15) states that SELF represents a point-of-view holder in a mental sense, while PIVOT represents a point-of-view holder in a physical sense, or "the center of deixis". He also notes in passing that PIVOT corresponds to the notion of "empathy" (p. 455, fn. 14). At the very least, it seems that the concept of PIVOT as envisioned by Sells is, by itself, a complex notion that encompasses multiple facets of logophoricity (see Oshima 2007; Charnavel 2014 for relevant discussion).

It is also worth mentioning in this connection that Culy (1997) argues, based on a crosslinguistic survey, that "logophoricity proper is distinct from point of view" (p. 846), citing cases in which logophoric pronouns do not represent points of view. He claims that logophoric pronouns and indirect (or long-distance) reflexives may indicate points of view but do so only secondarily, and the effect of this secondary function becomes visible in those contexts where the use of a logophoric form is optional. In such contexts, the use of a logophoric form in place of an ordinary pronoun is interpreted as representing the reported speaker's point of view. This means, then, that the presence of point-of-view effects is not a necessary condition for logophoricity, and, conversely, that the absence of point-of-view effects does not immediately exclude the possibility that a given expression is a logophor.

Hence, without committing myself to the view that all instances of logophoricity are reducible to point-of-view considerations, I use the term PIVOT only as a descriptive term to refer to a logocentric antecedent that is neither SOURCE nor SELF. But if there is no clear definition of PIVOT besides being neither SOURCE nor SELF, how can we identify logophoric environments in English to explore the hypothesis that names in English are maximally antilogophoric?

Instead of giving an elusive definition of PIVOT, I would like to adopt a heuristic approach here. Let us assume that logophoric pronouns in languages like Japanese, Ngiti, and Boko are maximally logophoric in the sense that they can take the widest range of logocentric antecedents (see Chapter 2). Let us assume then that if, in a given configuration, *x* can antecede a logophoric pronoun *y* in these languages, then *x* is identified as a potential logocentric antecedent for *y* in that configuration. If *x* is neither SOURCE nor SELF, it is PIVOT.

In what follows, I draw primarily from Japanese logophoric binding data to investigate the antilogophoric properties of names in English, and simply assume that essentially the same results can be replicated by using Ngiti and Boko logophoric pronouns. It should be emphasized, however, that I do not intend to claim that logophors in these languages pick out exactly the same set of logocentric antecedents in all contexts. Presumably there are independent (perhaps language-specific) restrictions on the selection of logocentric antecedents that are yet to be understood.

4.3. *Zibun* as a Tool for Locating Potential Logocentric Antecedents

This section is intended to provide justification for the use of Japanese *zibun* as a diagnostic tool for identifying potential logocentric antecedents.

As mentioned above, there is a view that locally bound *zibun* is a pure anaphor regulated in the syntax whereas long-distance bound *zibun* is a logophor subject to discourse-pragmatic constraints (Sells 1987a: 450, fn. 6; Abe 1997; cf. Oshima 2004, 2007; Kishida 2011 for a three-way classification of *zibun*). A rationale cited by Abe (1997) in support of this dichotomy is that, as observed by Kuno (1972, 1973), long-distance bound *zibun* generally exhibits "awareness" effects, while *zibun* in simplex sentences does not have to obey the awareness requirement.[9]

The notion of "awareness" (or "consciousness") is similar to point of view and is often invoked in the discussion of logophoricity. It has been recognized since Kuno (1972, 1973) that the use of Japanese *zibun* is subject to the so-called awareness requirement, and the same constraint has proven to be relevant to Mandarin *ziji* as well (Huang and Liu 2001). The basic idea is as follows.

(30) *Zibun* in a constituent clause [= an embedded clause] (A) is coreferential with a noun phrase (B) of the matrix sentence only if A represents an action or state that the referent of B is *aware of* at the time it takes place or has come to be aware of at some later time. In other words, *zibun* appears in subordinate clauses only when the clauses represent the internal feeling of the referent of *zibun* and the first pronoun appears in its place in the direct representation of the internal feeling.

(Kuno 1973: 322)

By way of illustration, compare the a-sentences with the b-sentences in (31) and (32) below. (Examples are taken from Kuno (1973: 309-310).)

(31) a. John$_1$-wa [Mary-ga zibun$_1$-o korosootosita toki] Jane-to
John-TOP Mary-NOM self-ACC tried.to.kill when Jane-with
nete ita.
sleeping was
'John$_1$ was in bed with Jane when Mary tried to kill him$_1$.'

b. *John$_1$-wa [Mary-ga zibun$_1$-o korosita toki] Jane-to
John-TOP Mary-NOM self-ACC killed when Jane-with
nete ita.
sleeping was
'John$_1$ was in bed with Jane when Mary killed him$_1$.'

---

[9] The same argument is employed by Huang and Liu (2001) in their analysis of Mandarin *ziji*.

(32) a. John₁-wa [_RC_ zibun₁-o korosootosita] sono okoto-to maeni
         John-TOP   self-ACC tried.to.kill the   man-with before
         atta koto-ga-atta.
         met ASP
         'John₁ had met before the man who tried to kill him₁.'
   b. *John₁-wa [_RC_ zibun₁-o korosita] sono okoto-to maeni atta
         John-TOP   self-ACC killed   the man-with before met
         koto-ga-atta.
         ASP
         'John₁ had met before the man who killed him₁.'

According to Kuno (1972, 1973), the unacceptability of the b-sentences in (31) and (32) follows from the fact that they fail to abide by the awareness requirement; that is, John could not have been aware that he was killed.

The awareness requirement seems to follow directly from the nature of logophoricity, but here again, opinions seem to diverge among researchers on how to interpret this notion. On Sells's account, awareness is distinguished from the notion of "point of view" (Sells 1987: 471), whereas on Abe's (1997) account, awareness is subsumed under point of view. In Huang and Liu (2001) and Oshima (2004), the awareness requirement is reinterpreted as _de se_ interpretation requirements.

Aside from the question of where the awareness requirement comes from, an interesting fact is that locally bound _zibun_ generally fails to show awareness effects. For example, in (33), _Mary_ can bind _zibun_, and the sentence does not mean that Mary was aware that she was killed in her own house.

(33) Mary₁-ga   John-ni   zibun₁-no uti-de   koros-are-ta.
      Mary-NOM   John-by   self-GEN house-LOC   kill-PASS-PAST
      'Mary₁ was killed by John in her₁ house.'
                                                    (Kuno 1973: 313)

The absence of awareness effects has sometimes been taken as evidence for the claim that _zibun_ taking a local antecedent is not a logophor but an anaphor subject to syntactic conditions. However, the presence/absence of awareness effects does not consistently correlate with the (non-)locality of the antecedent of _zibun_. As observed by Kuroda (1973), not all occurrences of long-distance bound *zibun* invariably display awareness effects. He points out that the following example, due to Kuno (1972: 184), is acceptable even in a context where John has a desire to marry someone who the speaker knows is his student, but who John does not realize is his own student (perhaps because he has so many students in his class).

(34) John₁-wa [_RC_ zibun₁-ga osie-teiru] gakusei to
John-TOP self-NOM teach-ASP student with
kekkonsi-tagatteiru-yo.
marry-want
'John₁ wants to marry a student who he₁ teaches.'

In a similar vein, for many speakers, the sentence in (35) below is felicitous in the following scenario: Mary does not know that she was abandoned immediately after birth, nor that the person who she works with is her natural parent, but the speaker knows that they are a parent and a child and that the colleague is the one who abandoned her.

(35) Mary₁-wa [_RC_ zibun₁-o suteta] oya-to issyoni
Mary-TOP self-ACC abandoned parent-with together
hatarai-teiru.
work-ASP
'Mary works with her parent who abandoned her.'

It should also be mentioned that unlike in the case of English local anaphors, certain predicates disallow local binding of *zibun* (Oshima 1979: 426).

(36) *Taroo₁-wa zibun₁-o korosita.
Taro-TOP self-ACC killed
'Taro killed himself.'

In view of the fact that the correlation between the remoteness of the antecedent of *zibun* and the occurrence of awareness effects breaks down in non-trivial ways, the absence of awareness effects does not immediately justify the claim that locally bound *zibun* is subject to a local binding condition. Note also that it might be possible to modulate the notion of locality in order to maintain the correlation (see Abe 1997), but even if the alleged correlation is real, we cannot hastily conclude that locally bound *zibun* must (unambiguously) be an anaphor. The fact that *zibun* "does not have to" adhere to the awareness requirement allows us to merely conclude that it *can* be an anaphor (and possibly ambiguous between an anaphor and a logophor), and to that extent, the jury is still out on whether it cannot be a logophor.[10] Thus, absent evidence to the contrary, let us assume that Japanese *zibun* (as well as Mandarin *ziji*) is always a logophor regardless of the distance of the antecedent (and may also be an anaphor in some restricted environments). This might strike one as a radical departure from the prevailing orthodoxy, but to claim that *zibun* (or *ziji*) must not be a logophor in a certain domain requires additional justification. The onus of proof is, therefore, on those who wish to make such a claim and draw a demarcation line between the domain in which *zibun* must behave as an anaphor and the domain in which *zibun* must behave as a logophor.[11]

---

[10] The difficulty in adjudicating on this issue comes in part from the fact that the antecedent of *zibun* must always denote a sentient individual. The same kind of complication can be avoided by using an inanimate antecedent in the case of, say, English *each other*, which is claimed to have an anaphoric and a logophoric use (Pollard and Sag 1992). Hence the contrast between (i) and (ii) below.

    (i) a. I placed the boys$_1$ next to each other$_1$.
        b. I placed the pens$_1$ next to each other$_1$.
    (ii) a. I placed the boys$_1$ next to each other$_1$'s mothers.
        b. #I placed the pens$_1$ next to each other$_1$'s cases.

(Drummond 2011: 180)

See Charnavel and Sportiche (2016) for a detailed investigation of French anaphors that aims to clarify the boundary between the domain in which an anaphor falls under Condition A and the domain in which it is exempt from the condition.

[11] My position is in part in line with Reinhart and Reuland's (1993) view. They state that:

    (i) the terms *local anaphor* and *long-distance anaphor* are highly misleading. Both kinds of anaphor can occur at all kinds of distances when they are used logophorically.

(Reinhart and Reuland 1993: 660)

Note, though, that Reinhart and Reuland distinguish between *perspective logophors* and *focus logophors*, claiming that only the latter can appear in coargument configurations, namely, contexts where an anaphoric expression and its antecedent are coarguments of the same predicate.

4.4. The Scope of Condition C

4.4.1. Condition C Revisited

We are now in a position to reconsider Condition C effects. Classic examples of Condition C effects are given below.

(37) a. *He$_1$ loves John$_1$'s mother.
 b. *He$_1$ told Mary that John$_1$ was going to see Bill.
 c. *He$_1$ told Mary that John was going to see Bill$_1$.
 d. *She$_1$ was told that Bill was looking for Mary$_1$.
 e. *We asked her$_1$ to bring Rosa$_1$'s pictures.
 f. *She$_1$ saw a man who approached Maria$_1$'s mother.
 g. *She$_1$ got mad because Frank criticized Rosa$_1$.

If the hypothesis outlined above is correct, all these examples fall under antilogophoricity restrictions because the relevant names are situated within the domain with respect to which the coreferential pronoun can be construed as the logophoric center. This is confirmed by the fact that Japanese allows binding of *zibun* in these configurations.

(38) a. Kare$_1$-wa zibun$_1$-no hahaoya-o aisiteiru.
   he-TOP self-GEN mother-ACC love
   (Lit.) 'He loves self's mother.'
 b. Kare$_1$-wa Mary-ni [zibun$_1$-ga Bill-ni au koto]-o
   he-TOP Mary-DAT self-NOM Bill-DAT meet COMP-ACC
   tutaeta.
   told
   (Lit.) 'He told Mary that self was going to see Bill.'
 c. Kare$_1$-wa Mary-ni [John-ga zibun$_1$-ni au koto]-o
   he-TOP Mary-DAT John-NOM self-DAT meet COMP-ACC
   tutaeta.
   told
   (Lit.) 'He told Mary that John was going to see self.'

d. Kanozyo$_1$-wa [Bill-ga zibun$_1$-o sagasiteiru koto]-o
   she-TOP Bill-NOM self-ACC was.looking.for COMP-ACC
   tutae-rare-ta.
   tell-PASS-PAST
   (Lit.) 'She was told that Bill was looking for self.'

e. Watasitati-wa kanozyo$_1$-ni [zibun$_1$-no syasin-o mottekuru
   we-TOP she-DAT self-GEN picture-ACC bring
   yooni] tanonda.
   AUX asked
   (Lit.) 'We asked her to bring self's pictures.'

f. Kanozyo$_1$-wa [$_{RC}$ zibun$_1$-no hahaoya-ni tikazuita] otoko-o
   she-TOP self-GEN mother-to approached man-ACC
   mita.
   saw
   (Lit.) 'She saw a man who approached self's mother.'

g. Kanozyo$_1$-wa [Frank-ga zibun$_1$-o hihansita kara] okotta.
   she-TOP Frank-NOM self-ACC criticized because got.mad
   (Lit.) 'She got mad because Frank criticized self.'

The following contrast may likewise be due to the proposed antilogophoricity constraint.

(39) a. *Near Dan$_1$, he$_1$ saw a snake.
     b. Near him$_1$, Dan$_1$ saw a snake.

In (39a), *he* serves as the logophoric center of *Dan*, whereas in (39b), *him* is presumably not a potential logophoric center for *Dan*. Again, support comes from logophoric binding data (from Japanese).

(40) a. Zibun$_1$-no tikaku-ni kare$_1$-wa hebi-o mituketa.
        self-GEN proximity-LOC he-TOP snake-ACC found
        (Lit.) 'In self's proximity, he saw a snake.'
     b. *Kare$_1$-no tikaku-ni zibun$_1$-wa hebi-o mituketa.
        he-GEN proximity-LOC self-TOP snake-ACC found
        (Lit.) 'In his proximity, self saw a snake.'

The contrast above shows that logocentric antecedence is not determined by linear order. By definition, Condition C is also not imposed on the linear relation between a pronoun and its antecedent. Thus, Condition C assumes no jurisdiction over coreference in sentences like those below, where the pronoun linearly precedes but does not c-command the R-expression that it corefers with.

(41) a. His$_1$ mother loves John$_1$.
b. Those who know him$_1$ hate Bill$_1$.

Note that antilogophoricity restrictions are also not applicable to sentences (41a–b) above. The pronouns *his* and *him* are not potential logophoric centers relative to *John* and *Bill*, as confirmed by the fact that *zibun*-binding fails in these configurations.

(42) a. *Kare$_1$-no hahaoya-wa zibun$_1$-o aisiteiru.
he-GEN mother-TOP self-ACC love
(Lit.) 'His mother loves self.'
b. *[Kare$_1$-o sitteiru] hito-wa zibun$_1$-o nikundeiru.
he-ACC know people-TOP self-ACC hate
(Lit.) 'People who know him hate self.'

Let us also take a look at the following examples, where antilogophoric effects are presumably operative.

(43) *We have heard from him$_1$ that Walter$_1$ will never be allowed to enter the Lodge.

(Sells 1987b: 6)

(44) *John's suicide meant to her$_1$ that Mary$_1$ had been betrayed by him.

Under the Condition C account, it must be claimed that the pronouns in (43) and (44) somehow c-command out of the PP in which they are embedded. Under the antilogophoricity account, on the other hand, the deviance of these examples can be attributed to violations of the antilogophoricity constraint. That *him* in (43) and *her* in (44) are potential logophoric centers is confirmed by the fact that *zibun*-binding is possible in the same contexts.

(45) Taroo-wa Takasi$_1$-kara [Yosiko-ga zibun$_1$-o nikundeiru
Taro-TOP Takashi-from Yoshiko-NOM LOG-ACC hate
to] kiita.
COMP heard

'Taro heard from Takashi₁ that Yoshiko hated him₁.'

(Sells 1987: 454)

(46) John-no   zisatu-wa   Mary₁-nitotte [zibun₁-ga   kare-ni
     John-GEN suicide-TOP Mary-to   LOG-NOM   he-by
     uragir-are-ta   koto]-o   imisita.
     betray-PASS-PAST COMP-ACC meant
     'John's suicide meant to Mary₁ that she₁ had been betrayed by him.'

(Kuno 1972: 190)

4.4.2. Intervention Effects

We have seen that Condition C and antilogophoricity restrictions are supposed to operate in significantly overlapping environments. This seems to mean that the question always remains as to whether observed Condition C effects are due to either Condition C or antilogophoricity restrictions or both.

However, there is a peculiar property of logophoric binding that helps adjudicate on this question. As we observed earlier, languages like Japanese impose far more lenient restrictions on logophoric binding than other languages. A point worth noting here is that not only is logophoric binding in such languages possible in a wide variety of contexts, but it is also (apparently) unbounded even in the presence of an intervener. Observe the following sentences.

(47) Taroo₁-wa [Hanako-ga   [zibun₁-ga   wairo-o   moratta
     Taro-TOP   Hanako-NOM self-NOM   bribe-ACC   receive
     koto]-o   Ziroo-ni   tugeta to]   omotteiru.
     COMP-ACC Jiro-DAT   told   COMP   think
     'Taro₁ thinks that Hanako told Jiro that he₁ had received a bribe.'

(48) [[Zibun₁-ga   wairo-o   moratta to]   Hanako-ga   sinziteiru
     self-NOM   bribe-ACC   receive   COMP Hanako-NOM believe
     koto]-ga   Taroo₁-o   nayamaseta.
     COMP-NOM Taro-ACC   distressed
     'The fact that Hanako believes that he₁ had received a bribe distressed Taro₁.'

In (47), *zibun* can be bound not only by the intermediate potential logocentric antecedent *Hanako* but also by the remote subject *Taroo*. Likewise, in (48), *zibun* can be bound not only by the subject of the immediately dominating clause (i.e., *Hanako*) but also by the experiencer object in the matrix clause (i.e., *Taroo*).

However, even in Japanese, where logophoric binding is apparently unbounded and free from intervention effects, there is a specific kind of configuration in which long-distance binding surrenders to intervention—a type of intervention which, to my knowledge, has gone unnoticed in the literature. Consider the following examples.

(49) a. ?*Taroo$_1$-wa [$_{RC}$ Ziroo-ga [zibun$_1$-ga wairo-o moratta
Taro-TOP Jiro-NOM self-NOM bribe-ACC received
koto]-o tugeta] hito-ni atta.
COMP-ACC told person-to meet
'Taro$_1$ met the person to whom Jiro said that he$_1$ received a bribe.'

b. ?*Taroo$_1$-wa [$_{RC}$ [zibun$_1$-ga makeru to] itta] gakusei-o
Taro-TOP self-NOM lose COMP said student-ACC
sikatta.
scolded
'Taro$_1$ scolded a student who said that he$_1$ would lose.'

c. ?*Takasi$_1$-wa [Taroo-ga iuniwa Yosiko-ga mizu-o
Takasi-TOP Taro-according.to Yoshiko-NOM water-ACC
zibun$_1$-no ue-ni kobosita node] nuretesimatta.
self-GEN on-LOC spilled because got.wet
'Takashi$_1$ got wet because according to Taro, Yoshiko spilled water on him$_1$.'

These sentences are unacceptable (or at best marginal) with the given coindexation. Note that long-distance binding into a relative clause or an adverbial itself is permitted in Japanese, as we witnessed earlier. The relevant examples are repeated here.

(50) Taroo$_1$-wa [$_{RC}$ zibun$_1$-ga moratta] okane-o tukatta.
Taro-TOP self-NOM received money-ACC used
'Taro$_1$ used the money that he$_1$ had received.'

(51) Takasi₁-wa [Yosiko-ga   mizu-o   zibun-₁no ue-ni   kobosita
     Takasi-TOP Yoshiko-NOM water-ACC self-GEN on-LOC   spilled
     node]   nuretesimatta.
     because got.wet
     'Takashi₁ got wet because Yoshiko spilled water on him₁.'

(Sells 1987a: 455)

Then what is it that makes the sentences in (49a–c) significantly degraded compared to (47) and (48)? The answer presumably lies in the fact that in the deviant cases, the remote antecedent is understood as the PIVOT, whereas in the good cases, the remote antecedent is understood as either the SOURCE or the SELF.

Note that for intervention to occur, it is not sufficient that the remote antecedent acts as the PIVOT. It is also required that the intervener be a SOURCE; otherwise, no intervention effects come about, as shown below.

(52) PIVOT > SELF > *zibun*
     Taroo₁-wa [[zibun₁-ga wairo-o   moratta   koto]-ga
     Taro-TOP   self-NOM   bribe-ACC received COMP-NOM
     Hanako-o   nayamaseta node] kaisya-o   satta.
     Hanako-ACC   disstressed because company-ACC left
     'Taro₁ left the company because the fact that he₁ had received a bribe distressed Hanako.'

(53) PIVOT > PIVOT > *zibun*
     Taroo₁-wa [Hanako-ga   [_RC zibun₁-ga moratta] okane-o
     Taro-TOP Hanako-NOM   self-NOM received money-ACC
     tukattesimatta node]   ryokoo-ni ik-e-nakat-ta.
     used   because travel-to go-can-NEG-PAST
     'Taro₁ couldn't go traveling because Hanako used the money he₁ had received.'

In (52) and (53), *zibun* can be bound by the remote PIVOT antecedent in spite of the presence of an intervening potential logocentric antecedent. The fact that no intervention effects occur in these cases suggests that it is only SOURCE that can thwart the binding of *zibun* to a remote PIVOT antecedent.

So far we have examined the following cases.

(54) a. ^{OK}SOURCE > SOURCE > *zibun*   (e.g., (47))
     b. ^{OK}SELF > SOURCE > *zibun*   (e.g., (48))
     c. *PIVOT > SOURCE > *zibun*   (e.g., (49))
     d. ^{OK}PIVOT > SELF > *zibun*   (e.g., (52))
     e. ^{OK}PIVOT > PIVOT > *zibun*   (e.g., (53))

To confirm whether there is any other intervention configuration than (54c), let us examine all the other logically possible configurations.[12]

(55) SOURCE > SELF > *zibun*
     Taroo$_1$-wa [[zibun$_1$-ga wairo-o moratta koto]-ga
     Taro-TOP   self-NOM   bribe-ACC receive COMP-NOM
     Hanako-o   nayamaseta to]   Ziroo-ni tugeta.
     Hanako-ACC distressed   COMP Jiro-DAT told
     'Taro$_1$ told Jiro that the fact that he$_1$ had received a bribe distressed Hanako.'

(56) SOURCE > PIVOT > *zibun*
     Taroo$_1$-wa [Hanako-ga   [$_{RC}$ zibun$_1$-ga moratta] okane-o
     Taro-TOP   Hanako-NOM   self-NOM received money-ACC
     tukattesimatta koto]-o   Ziroo-ni tugeta.
     used   COMP-ACC Jiro-DAT told
     'Taro$_1$ told Jiro that Hanako used the money that he$_1$ had received.'

(57) SELF > SELF > *zibun*
     [[Zibun$_1$-ga wairo-o   moratta koto]-ga   Hanako-o
       self-NOM   bribe-ACC received COMP-NOM Hanako-ACC
     kanasimaseta koto]-ga   Taroo$_1$-o nayamaseta.
     saddened   COMP-NOM Taro-ACC distressed
     'The fact that the fact that he$_1$ had received a bribe saddened Hanako distressed Taro$_1$.'

---

[12] Some of the examples presented here are not perfectly natural presumably for processing reasons, but crucially, all the examples are significantly better than those in (49).

(58) SELF > PIVOT > *zibun*
[[$_{RC}$ Zibun$_1$-ga moratta] okane-o Hanako-ga tukattesimatta
self-NOM received money-ACC Hanako-NOM used
koto]-ga Taroo$_1$-o nayamaseta.
COMP-NOM Taro-ACC distressed
'The fact that Hanako used the money that he$_1$ had received distressed Taro$_1$.'

The sentences in (55)–(58) contrast sharply with (49a–c) in terms of acceptability.

To sum up, Japanese logophoric binding is quite permissible but is not always unbounded; binding by a PIVOT antecedent fails in the presence of an intervening SOURCE. Let us call this particular intervention context the *supreme intervention configuration*.

(59) *Supreme Intervention Configuration*
[PIVOT ... [SOURCE [... *zibun* ...] ...] ...]

Now, given that *zibun* is maximally logophoric, and given that names in English are at the opposite end of the spectrum, it is expected that antilogophoric restrictions are suspended in the following configuration (provided that other confounding factors are appropriately controlled for).

(60) [PIVOT ... [SOURCE [... *name* ...] ...] ...]

The underlying idea here is that since the supreme intervention configuration creates a context maximally immune to logophoric effects, such a context is expected to serve as a sanctuary for antilogophoric expressions. If putative Condition C effects disappear in the above configuration, there is good reason to believe that the observed disjoint-reference effects are attributed not to Condition C but to antilogophoricity restrictions alone because Condition C is supposed to apply irrespective of the presence or absence of an intervening SOURCE.

If we look at actual data, we see Condition C effects vanish (or significantly diminish) in the configuration above. O'Grady (2005) presents some naturally occurring examples from spoken and written discourse in which

Condition C is apparently violated. Some of his examples are given below.

(61) a. He₁ was shot in the arm when, police say, Sua₁ lunged at them.
[report on the Channel 8 News, Honolulu, February 7, 1997]
b. President Boris Yeltsin today canceled all meetings for this week because of medical tests for his upcoming heart surgery. He₁ also punished a former bodyguard who said Yeltsin₁ was too sick to govern.
[AP story in the *Honolulu Star-Bulletin*, Oct. 28, 1996]
c. He₁ reserved special scorn for a critic who wrote that Balthus₁ had been deeply influenced by the art of Germany, during a youthful period spent in that country.
['The Balthus Enigma' by Nicholas Weber, *The New Yorker*, Sept. 6, 1999, p. 36]

Casting doubt on the existence of Condition C as a grammatical principle, O'Grady argues that so-called Condition C effects are attributed to pragmatic and processing factors. Under his approach, the well-formedness of the examples cited above is attributed to the fact that the c-commanding pronoun and the relevant R-expression are separated by certain distance. To quote O'Grady:

(62) [T]he sentences are so long that at the point where the pronoun is used, the speaker cannot anticipate the need for a nominal later in the utterance to reactivate the referent. Or, alternatively, by the time the speaker reaches the part of the sentence where the nominal is used, he or she can no longer recall having used a pronoun earlier in the utterance.

(O'Grady 2005: 53)

It is true that the absence of Condition C effects in the sentences in (61) poses a serious problem for any approach that posits Condition C as an absolute structural condition disallowing coreference between an R-expression and a c-commanding pronoun. However, the claim that Condition C effects can be traced to processing considerations is highly suspect; for it is not the case that just any kind of "long" intervening material will remove disjoint-reference effects. The following sentence, for instance, does not improve at all even though the c-commanding pronoun and its antecedent are separated by a series of intervening phrases.

(63) *He₁ has told me in a very sad tone that as soon as the semester began John₁ was kicked out of school.

In my view, the key to the mysterious ameliorating effects in (61) lies in the fact that in all those examples, there is a SOURCE that intervenes between a pronoun that is understood as the PIVOT and a name that the pronoun is coreferential with. In (61a), *he* is understood as the PIVOT, and *police* acts an intervening SOURCE. In (61b), *he* is understood as the PIVOT, and *a former bodyguard* acts as an intervening SOURCE. In (61c), *he* is understood as the PIVOT, and *a critic* is an intervening SOURCE. Thus, the examples in (61) can be schematically represented in the following way.

(61a)′ [He   ...   [police   ...   [Sua   ...]]]
       PIVOT   SOURCE   name

(61b)′ [He   ...   [a former bodyguard ...   [Yeltsin ...]]]
       PIVOT   SOURCE   name

(61c)′ [He   ...   [a critic   ...   [Balthus ...]]]
       PIVOT   SOURCE   name

The intervention account outlined above offers a unified explanation of the otherwise unexpected acceptability of these sentences. That is, due to the presence of the intervening SOURCE, the PIVOT pronoun is hindered from searching into the logophoric domain that falls under the scope of the intervener. This is why antilogophoric effects fail to surface here.

O'Grady gives two more examples (given below).

(64) a. Lawrence crammed for Miami as if it were a final exam: he₁ hired a Spanish tutor, who placed new words on little note cards around Lawrence₁'s house...
    ['The Herald's Cuban Revolution' by Mimi Swartz, *The New Yorker*, June 1, 1999, p. 40]
  b. He₁'s far enough ahead that, if everything fell just right, Jarret₁ could be the champion when the checkered flag waves at the end of the 500-kilometer, 312-lap race.
    [AP story in the *Honolulu Advertiser*, Nov. 7, 1999, p. C11]

Apparently, there is no intervening SOURCE in these cases, but I argue that these examples are also compatible with the antilogophoricity account. In (64a), *Lawrence* is placed within a non-restrictive relative clause. As mentioned in the previous chapter, a non-restrictive phrase is essentially an inserted comment by the speaker of the utterance, which means that *Lawrence* is outside the logophoric domain of the pronoun *he*. Thus, the antilogophoricity constraint can be circumvented here. In (64b), the parenthetical *if*-clause intervenes between the c-commanding pronoun and *Jarret*. Since parentheticals are used to add the external speaker's comment or judgment on the described event, it is plausible to assume that in this sentence, the speaker is presented as a "secondary ego", i.e., a secondary internal SOURCE. Notice that the coreferring pronoun here is the PIVOT. This suggests, then, that the acceptability of the sentence in (64b) can also be attributed to intervention.

The intervention account receives further empirical support from the fact that Condition C effects disappear (or diminish) precisely in the configuration represented in (60). In other words, disjoint-reference effects persist when the sentence does not match the configuration. The following sentences, for example, are reported to be unacceptable even though there is an intervening SOURCE.

(65) *The claim that John said that Bill$_1$ was a spy was made by him$_1$.

(Kuno 2004: 332)

(66) *That John$_1$ was in love with her, he$_1$ claimed that Mary believed.

(Kuno 1987: 108)

In (65), the offending pronoun is the SOURCE with respect to the content of the complement clause of *claim*. Similarly, in (66), the pronoun *he* is understood as the SOUCE relative to the propositional complement of *claimed*. In these cases, the antilogophoricity constraint comes into play, forcing the names to be disjoint in reference from logocentric arguments.

These facts are quite telling because they at once vindicate the antilogophoricity hypothesis under consideration and disconfirm the relevance of Condition C to what have normally been conceived of as Condition C effects. Were Condition C at work in the intervention configuration, disjoint-reference effects should persist irrespective of the presence of an intervening

SOURCE.

Since Sells (1987b) addresses a similar issue, let us now take a look at his data and analysis. Based primarily on McCray's (1980) observations, Sells attempts to shed light on the discourse factors responsible for the "unexpected" acceptability of backward anaphora. McCray observed that Condition C effects can be mitigated under certain conditions. Some of her examples are given below.

(67) a. ?*It was pointed out to him$_1$ that Walter$_1$ was unsuccessful.
  b. It was rather indelicately pointed out to him$_1$ that Walter$_1$ would never become a successful accountant.

(McCray 1980: 331)

(68) She$_1$ was told that under no circumstances would Mary$_1$ have to compromise herself.

(McCray 1980: 334)

(69) It was pointed out to him$_1$ that sitting directly to the right of Walter$_1$ was the man he had just maligned.

(McCray 1980: 334)

Let us first examine (67a) and (67b). Sells (1987b: 14) claims that what is responsible for the contrast between (67a) and (67b) is the fact that in the former, "the reference time in the embedded clause is the 'current' reference time for Walter" (p. 14). By contrast, in the latter, the event described in the embedded clause is "not yet realized relative to the time of the pointing out, and thus will not be from Walter's point of view" (pp. 14–15), which, according to Sells, has the effect of drawing a discourse-role off *Walter*. What is more important in my view, however, is the presence of the phrase "rather indelicately" in (67b). This phrase is used here to express the speaker's judgment on the event, which suggests that the speaker is internalized as a secondary SOURCE. Since the pronoun *him* in this sentence is understood as the PIVOT relative to the embedded proposition, and since the internalized SOURCE acts as an intervener, (67b) involves an environment opaque to logophoric effects. Hence the name *Walter* survives even though the preceding pronoun is anaphoric to it.

Let us next consider (68) and (69). Sells observes that there is a contrast between (70a–b), on the one hand, and (71a–b), on the other, and suggests that the unexpected ameliorating effect can only occur when the pronoun is a non-SOURCE argument.

(70) a. *He₁ has heard from us that Walter ₁will be allowed to enter the Lodge.
 b. He₁ has heard from us that under no circumstances will Walter₁ be allowed to enter the Lodge.

(71) a. *We have heard from him₁ that Walter₁ will be allowed to enter the Lodge.
 b. *We have heard from him₁ that under no circumstances will Walter₁ be allowed to enter the Lodge.

The fact that (71b) does not improve is expected under the intervention account, too, because intervention occurs only when the relevant pronoun is understood as a PIVOT. What might at first sight seem puzzling is that in (68), (69), and (70b), there are no explicit intervening SOURCEs. I argue, however, that there is more than meets the eye here.

Before presenting my own analysis of these sentences, let us look at Sells's (1987b) account. Regarding (70b), Sells claims that *under no circumstances* is a SOURCE-oriented phrase, so that it "confirms *us* as the SOURCE in the embedded clause" (p. 12). Since being a SOURCE entails being also a SELF as well as a PIVOT, "the explicit marking of the presence of a SOURCE that is distinct from the 'target' referent" reconfirms that "Walter cannot be understood as linked to any of the potential role-predicates" (*ibid.*). As for (69), Sells states that the sentence is acceptable because"[t]he specification of Walter's location relative to the man is not taken from the sentence-internal viewpoint" (p. 16).

Unlike Sells, I argue that the crucial factor for the acceptability of (68), (69), and (70b) has bearing on the fact that they involve embedded inversion. Specifically, I claim that inversion in embedded contexts also serves to internalize the current speaker as a secondary SOURCE of the report. Evidence in support of this claim comes from Green's (1976) observation that inversion in embedded clauses is possible just in case the speaker agrees with or endorses the content of the embedded proposition. The following contrasts in (72) and (73) illustrate this point.

(72) a. John says that never before have prices been so high, and I agree.
b. *John says that never before have prices been so high, and I disagree/but he's wrong.

(Green 1976: 386)

(73) a. John says that standing in the corner is a man with a camera, and I think he's right.
b. *John says that standing in the corner is a man with a camera, but he's wrong.

(Green 1976: 386)

The facts shown here provide independent justification for the claim that embedded inversion introduces the current speaker as a secondary SOURCE in the discourse. This is also supported by Dorgeloh's (1997) view that inversion in embedded contexts "makes it evident to the hearer or reader that the speaker himself, though not overtly the subject of the discourse reported, does at least not dissociate himself from the content expressed" (p. 100). If so, McCray's examples in (68) and (69) are also subsumed under the intervention account. That is, both (68) and (69) involve an implicit SOURCE that intervenes between the PIVOT pronoun and the R-expression it is anaphoric to.[13] Hence *Mary* and *Walter* escape antilogophoricity restrictions. In the same vein, the data in (70) and (71) receive a straightforward explanation; that is, of the four sentences in (70a–b) and (71a–b), only (70b) meets the supreme intervention configuration. All the other examples, by contrast, do not involve intervention, thereby coming under the control of the antilogophoricity constraint.

Let us consider one more pair of sentences from McCray (1980).

(74) a. *He$_1$ didn't give her a diamond ring because Walter$_1$ isn't ready.
b. He$_1$ didn't give her a diamond ring because, although he's madly in love with her, Walter$_1$'s just not ready to tie the knot.

(McCray 1980: 331)

---

[13] Dubinsky and Hamilton (1998) analyze the subject of the verb *hear* and the indirect object of *tell* as falling under the category of SELF. However, these are considered to be PIVOTs if we follow Sells (1987a: 465, fn. 24) and Sells (1987b: 5).

Here again, certain intervening material renders otherwise illicit backward coreference possible. The contrast is no longer puzzling, however. The crucial difference between (74a) and (74b) is that the latter contains a parenthetical adverbial. As I argued above, parentheticals serve to introduce the current speaker of the utterance as a secondary internal SOURCE. If so, the acceptability of (74b) comes as no surprise because the intervening SOURCE makes the domain that contains *Walter* opaque to the PIVOT *he*. This is why no antilogophoric effects ensue here.

Summing up, we have looked at those contexts where both Condition C and antilogophoricity restrictions may in principle apply, and have examined whether Condition C effects persist if the antilogophoricity constraint is suspended. We have found that putative Condition C effects are voided when the effects of antilogophoricity restrictions are suppressed, which cannot be accounted for if we assume that Condition C and antilogophoricity restrictions apply simultaneously. What this suggests is that where the two disjointness conditions are both in principle applicable, only antilogophoricity restrictions are at work.

One might be tempted to leap to the conclusion that Condition C does not exist or that it is reducible to antilogophoricity restrictions. However, as we observed at the beginning of this chapter, there is good reason to believe that a disjointness condition like Condition C is necessary, independently of antilogophoricity restrictions. Recall the following examples.

(75) a. *It$_1$ is more famous than the designer of Royce Hall$_1$.
  b. Royce Hall$_1$ is more famous than its$_1$ designer.
  c. Its$_1$ designer is more famous than Royce Hall$_1$.

(76) a. *In 2002, they relocated it$_1$ to Myers Inc.$_1$'s current location
  b. In 2002, they relocated Myers Inc.$_1$ to its$_1$ current location.

(77) a. *It$_1$ was closed because a snow storm hit UCLA$_1$.
  b. Its$_1$ library was closed because a snow storm hit UCLA$_1$.

Given the standard assumption that inanimate DPs do not qualify as logocentric antecedents, the fact that disjointness effects arise in these cases indicates that we need Condition C (or some disjointness condition that does essentially the same job).

To reconcile the need for Condition C with the intervention facts we observed, it seems necessary to postulate a division of labor between antilogophoricity restrictions and Condition C in the production of so-called Condition C effects. Certainly, this requires a radical rethinking of the way Condition C is computed, and the question is how the division of labor between the two conditions should be implemented. At this stage, I can only speculate that there is an independent principle such that if the two disjointness conditions are both in principle applicable, antilogophoricity restrictions must be invoked. While further investigation is required to address this issue, it has become clear that the scope of Condition C is smaller than standardly assumed.

4.5. Summary

In this chapter, we closely reexamined what we normally regard as Condition C violations, with a view to confirming whether their ungrammaticality stems from Condition C or antilogophoricity restrictions. Close inspection revealed that so-called Condition C effects can be voided precisely in those contexts where logophoric binding in Japanese is preempted by intervention.

The findings reported here make a striking case for the hypothesis that names are maximally antilogophoric, while at the same time suggesting that Condition C is not always responsible for what we call Condition C effects.

Although Condition C and antilogophoricity restrictions are presumably independent constraints on coreference, the two disjointness conditions complement each other to give rise to disjoint-reference effects.

Chapter 5

Conclusion

Through the two case studies presented in this book, I have uncovered some of the core properties of antilogophoricity in natural language, and, by so doing, have delineated the sources of certain disjoint-reference effects that have not been properly investigated.

Below I summarize the major findings of the present study. First, I have shown that just as logophoricity comes in different types, antilogophoricity comes in different types, confirming Sells's (1987b) and Dubinsky and Hamilton's (1998) hypotheses from a new perspective. Specifically, names and epithets exhibit different degrees of antilogophoricity, which can be characterized as follows.

(1) Types of Antilogophoricity
    a. Names are maximally antilogophoric in the sense that they must be disjoint in reference from all potential logocentric antecedents (SOURCE, SELF, and PIVOT).
    b. Epithets are moderately antilogophoric in the sense that they must be disjoint in reference from a subset of logocentric antecedents (SOURCE and SELF).

Second, I have shown that there are two ways to escape antilogophoric effects.

(2) Antilogophoric restrictions can be circumvented by:
   (a) placing an antilogophor in an appositive phrase, or
   (b) placing an antilogophor in intervention contexts.

I have also shown that the apposition strategy in (2a) is hard to detect if the language being investigated has the option of adjoining an appositive phrase to a null pronominal. As for the intervention strategy in (2b), I have unveiled the existence of a (to my knowledge) previously undocumented type of intervention by capitalizing on maximally logophoric pronouns. The intervention configuration discovered is schematically represented as follows.

(3) *Supreme Intervention Configuration*
   [PIVOT ... [SOURCE [... *antilogophor* ...] ...] ...]

In the above configuration, the intervening SOURCE renders its logophoric domain opaque to the remote PIVOT, thereby voiding otherwise expected antilogophoric effects.

Third, I have shown that antilogophoricity and Binding Conditions conspire to obscure the sources of disjointness. As previously reported in the literature, epithets are subject to a type of antilogophoricity restriction and Binding Condition B, whose combined forces give the false impression that they obey Condition C. I have shown that this conspiracy is further obscured in a language like Japanese, where a null pronoun can be juxtaposed with an appositive epithet phrase.

As for names, we first observed that antilogophoricity restrictions and Condition C are independently motivated. Then, with a view to clarifying the scope of each condition, we looked into those cases where both Condition C and antilogophoricity restrictions may in principle apply.

(4)

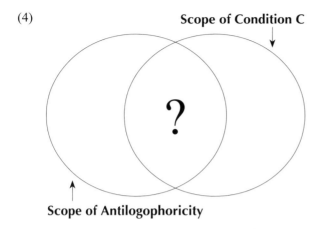

The picture that has emerged from the results of the present study is far from what one would normally envision. I have presented evidence suggesting the possibility that there is a division of labor between the two disjointness conditions, although they are presumably independent constraints on coreference.

(5)

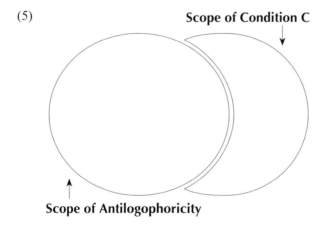

The findings of the present study indicate that the domain of Condition C must be smaller than standardly assumed. This conclusion itself raises perplexing questions. If the disjointness conditions actually operate in a way suggested here, the question immediately arises as to how this knowledge, which does not seem inductively inferable from experience, can be acquired. I have suggested that there seems to be an independent principle such that if the two disjointness conditions are both in principle applicable, antilogophoricity restrictions must be invoked. But the question remains — why should there be such a principle?

I would not dare to claim that the present work has unlocked all the mysteries of disjointness phenomena. Evidently, there are loose ends that need to be tied up, and, aside from the question raised above, there are intriguing questions that have arisen. Some of the remaining issues and open questions that are of particular importance are as follows.

(6) a. Why are epithets and names antilogophoric?
b. Why are there different kinds of (anti)logophoricity? And how many kinds are there?
c. How many kinds of intervention effects are there? Why should intervention effects exist?

Question (6a) is directly related to the fundamental question of why antilogophoricity should exist in natural language. It seems plausible to speculate that the antilogophoric nature of epithets is tied to the fact that they carry evaluative meanings, but then the question arises as to why names are also antilogophoric. As for (6b), it is worthwhile to investigate whether there is crosslinguistic variation in antilogophoricity. Likewise, it is also worth examining whether all types of R-expressions (including definite descriptions and demonstratives) are equally antilogophoric. As for (6c), it has been reported that exempt anaphors exhibit intervention effects of the kind different from what we saw. In Pollard and Sag (1992), intervention effects are viewed as processing-related phenomena, but whether (all) intervention effects are actually reduced to processing-based factors is still an open question. I leave all these questions for future research.

While there is still a long way to go, it is hoped that the present study contributes to the task of unraveling the tangled skein of factors behind the formidable variety of anaphoric patterns in natural languages.

References

Abe, Jun. 1992. The nature of anaphors and distributivity. ms., University of Connecticut.
Abe, Jun. 1997. The locality of *zibun* and logophoricity. In *Researching and verifying an advanced theory of human language*, COE research report (1), Graduate School of Language Sciences, Kanda University of International Studies, 595–626.
Abbott, Edwin Abbott. 1869. *A Shakespearian grammar: An attempt to illustrate some of the differences between Elizabethan and Modern English*. London: Macmillan.
Anderson, Stephen. 1986. The typology of anaphoric dependencies: Icelandic (and other) reflexives. In *Topics in Scandinavian syntax*, eds. Lars Hellan and Kirsti Koch Kristensen, 65–88. Dordrecht: Reidel.
Aoun, Joseph, and Lina Choueiri. 2000. Epithets. *Natural Language and Linguistic Theory* 18: 1–39.
Aoun, Joseph, Lina Choueiri, and Norbert Hornstein. 2001. Resumption, movement, and derivational economy. *Linguistic Inquiry* 32: 371–403.
Aoun, Joseph, and Norbert Hornstein. 1992. Bound and referential pronouns. In *Logical structure and linguistics structure: Cross-linguistic perspectives*, eds. C.-T. James Huang and Robert May, 1–23. Dordrecht: Kluwer.
Ariel, Mira. 1990. *Accessing noun-phrase antecedents*. London: Routledge.
Ariel, Mira. 1994. Interpreting anaphoric expressions: A cognitive versus a pragmatic approach. *Journal of Linguistics* 30: 3–42.
Battistella, Edwin. 1989. Chinese reflexivization: A movement to INFL approach. *Linguistics* 27: 987–1012.
Bolinger, Dwight. 1979. Pronouns in discourse. In *Syntax and semantics, vol. 12:*

Discourse and syntax, ed. Talmy Givón, 289–309. New York: Academic Press.
Bond, Oliver. 2006. A broader perspective on point of view: Logophoricity in Ogonoid languages. In *Selected Proceedings of the 35th Annual Conference on African Linguistics*, eds. John Mugane, John P. Hutchison, and Dee A. Worman, 234–244. Somerville, MA.: Cascadilla Proceedings Project.
Bruening, Benjamin. 2014. Precede-and-command revisited. *Language* 90: 342–388.
Büring, Daniel. 2005. *Binding theory*. Cambridge: Cambridge University Press.
Charnavel, Isabelle. 2014. Perspectives on binding and exemption. Paper presented at *MIT Ling-Lunch*, November 13, 2014.
Charnavel, Isabelle, and Dominique Sportiche. 2016. Anaphor binding: What French inanimate anaphors show. *Linguistic Inquiry* 47: 35–87.
Chomsky, Noam. 1981. *Lectures on government and binding*. Dordrecht: Foris.
Chomsky, Noam. 1986. *Knowledge of language*. New York: Praeger.
Chomsky, Noam. 1993. A minimalist program for linguistic theory. In *The view from building 20: Essays in linguistics in honor of Sylvain Bromberger*, eds. by Kenneth Hale and Samuel Jay Keyser, 1–52. Cambridge, MA.: MIT Press.
Chomsky, Noam. 1995. *The minimalist program*. Cambridge, MA.: MIT Press.
Chomsky, Noam, and Howard Lasnik. 1993. The theory of principles and parameters. In *Syntax: An international handbook of contemporary research*, eds. Joachim Jacobs, Arnim von Stechow, Wolfgang Sternefeld, and Theo Vennemann, 506–569. Berlin: Walter de Gruyter.
Clements, George Nicholas. 1974. Super-Equi and the intervention constraint. In *Papers from the 5th Annual Meeting of the North-Eastern Linguistic Society*, eds. Ellen Kaisse and Jorge Hankamer, 13–28. Cambridge, MA.: Harvard University.
Clements, George Nicholas. 1975. The logophoric pronoun in Ewe: Its role in discourse. *Journal of West African Languages* 10: 141–177.
Collins, Chris. 2005. A smuggling approach to the passive in English. *Syntax* 8: 81–120.
Collins, Chris, and Paul Martin Postal. 2012. *Imposters: A study of pronominal agreement*. Cambridge, MA.: MIT Press.
Conroy, Stacey, Eri Takahashi, Jeff Lidz, and Colin Phillips. 2009. Equal treatment for all antecedents: How children succeed with Principle B. *Linguistic Inquiry* 40: 446–486.
Corazza, Eros. 2013. Empathy as a psychological guide to the *de se*/*de re* distinction. In *Attitudes de se: Linguistics, epistemology, metaphysics*, eds. Neil Feit and Alessandro Capone, 211–234. Stanford, CA: CSLI Publications.
Culy, Christopher. 1994. Aspects of logophoric marking. *Linguistics* 32: 1055–1094.
Culy, Christopher. 1997. Logophoric pronouns and point of view. *Linguistics* 35: 845–59.
Culy, Christopher. 2002. The logophoric hierarchy and variation in Dogon. In *Reported discourse: A meeting ground for different linguistic domains*, eds. Tom Güldemann and Manfred von Roncador, 201–210. Amsterdam: John Benjamins.
Déchaine, Rose-Marie, and Martina Wiltschko. 2002. Decomposing pronouns. *Lin-*

guistic Inquiry 33: 409–442.
Dorgeloh, Heidrun. 1997. *Inversion in modern English: Form and function*. Amsterdam: John Benjamins.
Drummond, Alex. 2011. *Binding phenomena within a reductionist theory of grammatical dependencies*. Ph.D. dissertation, University of Maryland, College Park.
Dubinsky, Stanley, and Robert Hamilton. 1998. Epithets as antilogophoric pronouns. *Linguistic Inquiry* 29: 685–693.
Elbourne, Paul. 2005. *Situations and individuals*. Cambridge, MA.: MIT Press.
Emonds, Joseph. 1979. Appositive relatives have no properties. *Linguistic Inquiry* 10: 211–243.
Evans, Gareth. 1977. Pronouns, quantifiers and relative clauses (I). *Canadian Journal of Philosophy* 7: 467–536.
Freidin, Robert. 1992. *Foundations of generative syntax*. Cambridge, MA.: MIT Press.
Givón, Talmy. 1983. *Topic continuity in discourse: A quantitative cross-language study*. Amsterdam: John Benjamins.
Green, Georgia M. 1976. Main clause phenomena in subordinate clauses. *Language* 56: 382–397.
Greenberg, Joseph. 1963. Some universals of grammar with particular reference to the order of meaningful elements. In *Universals of language*, ed. Joseph Greenberg, 58–90. Cambridge, MA.: MIT Press.
Grinder, John T. 1970. Super Equi-NP deletion. *Papers from the Sixth Regional Meeting Chicago Linguistic Society*, 297–317.
Grodzinsky, Yosef, and Tanya Reinhart. 1993. The innateness of binding and coreference. *Linguistic Inquiry* 24: 69–101.
Hagège, Claude. 1974. Les pronoms logophoriques. *Bulletin de la Société de Linguistique de Paris* 69: 287–310.
Haïk, Isabelle. 1984. Indirect binding. *Linguistic Inquiry* 15: 185–223.
Hara, Takaaki. 2002. Bound variable interpretation and the degree of accessibility. In *Proceedings of ConSOLE IX*, eds. Marjo van Koppen, Erica Thrift, Erik Jan van der Torre, and Malte Zimmermann, 82–95. Leiden: SOLE.
Heim, Irene. 1998. Anaphora and semantic interpretation: A reinterpretation of Reinhart's approach. In *The interpretive tract. MIT Working Papers in Linguistics* 25, eds. Uli Sauerland, and Orin Percus, 205–246. Cambridge, MA.: MITWPL, Department of Linguistics and Philosophy, MIT.
Higginbotham, James. 1983. Logical form, binding, and nominals. *Linguistic Inquiry* 14: 395–420.
Higginbotham, James. 1985. On semantics. *Linguistic Inquiry* 16: 547–593.
Hinds, John. 1971. Personal pronouns in Japanese. *Glossa* 5: 146–155.
Hinds, John. 1975. Third person pronouns in Japanese. In *Language in Japanese society*, ed. Fred C.C. Peng, 129–157. Tokyo: University of Tokyo Press.
Hinds, John. 1978. Anaphora in Japanese conversation. In *Anaphora in discourse*, ed. John Hinds, 136–179. Alberta: Linguistic Research Inc.

Hoji, Hajime. 1990. Theories of anaphora and aspects of Japanese syntax. ms., University of Southern California.
Hoji, Hajime. 1991. Kare. In *Interdisciplinary approaches to language: Essays in honor of S.-Y. Kuroda*, eds. Carol J. Georgopoulos and Roberta Ishihara, 287–304. Dordrecht: Kluwer.
Hoji, Hajime. 1995. Demonstrative binding and Principle B. In *Proceedings of North East Linguistic Society* 25, ed. Jill N. Beckman, 255–271. Amherst, MA.: GLSA.
Hoji, Hajime. 1997. Sloppy identity and Principle B. In *Atomism and binding*, eds. Hans Bennis, Pierre Pica, and Johan Rooryck, 205–234. Dordrecht: Foris.
Hoji, Hajime, Satoshi Kinsui, Yukinori Takubo, and Ayumi Ueyama. 2000. Demonstratives, bound variables, and reconstruction effects. In *Proceedings of GLOW in ASIA II*, 141–158. Nagoya: Nansan University.
Hornstein, Norbert, and Amy Weinberg. 1990. The necessity of LF. *The Linguistic Review* 7: 129–168.
Huang, C.-T. James, and C.-S. Luther Liu. 2001. Logophoricity, attitudes and *ziji* at the interface. In *Syntax and semantics, vol. 33: Long-distance reflexives*, eds. Peter Cole, Gabriella Hermon, and C.-T. James Huang, 141–96. San Diego: Academic Press.
Huang, Yan. 2000. *Anaphora: A cross-linguistic study*. Oxford: Oxford University Press.
Hyman, Larry M., and Bernard Comrie. 1981. Logophoric reference in Gokana. *Journal of African Languages and Linguistics* 3: 19–37.
Inoue, Kazuko. 1976. *Henkei bunpoo to Nihongo* [Transformational grammar and Japanese]. Tokyo: Taishukan.
Jackendoff, Ray. 1972. *Semantic interpretation in generative grammar*. Cambridge, MA.: MIT Press.
Jespersen, Otto. 1949. *A modern English grammar on historical principles, Part VII: Syntax*. London: George Allen & Unwin.
Jones, Ross. 1998. *The Boko/Busa language cluster*. Munich: Lincom Europa.
Jones, Ross. 2000. Coreference marking in Boko—Logophoricity or not? *Journal of African Language and Linguistics* 21: 135–159.
Kanzaki, Takaaki. 1994. *Nichieigo daimeisi no kenkyuu* [A study of pronouns in Japanese and English]. Tokyo: Kenkyusya.
Kameyama, Megumi. 1985. *Zero anaphora: The case of Japanese*. Ph.D. dissertation, Stanford University.
Katada, Fusa. 1991. The LF representation of anaphors. *Linguistic Inquiry* 22: 287–313.
Kayne, Richard. 1994. *The antisymmetry of syntax*. Cambridge, MA.: MIT Press.
Keenan, Edward. 1971. Names, quantifiers, and the sloppy identity problem. *Research on Language and Social Interaction* 4, 211–232.
Kishida, Maki. 2011. *Reflexives in Japanese*. Ph.D. dissertation, University of Maryland, College Park.
Kitagawa, Chisato. 1981. Anaphora in Japanese: *Kare* and *zibun*. In *Coyote Papers*

2, eds. Ann K. Farmer and Chisato Kitagawa, 61–75. Tucson: University of Arizona.
Koopman, Hilda, and Dominique Sportiche. 1989. Pronouns, logical variables, and logophoricity in Abe. *Linguistic Inquiry* 20: 555–588.
Kuno, Susumu. 1972. Pronominalization, reflexivization, and direct discourse. *Linguistic Inquiry* 3: 161–195.
Kuno, Susumu. 1973. *The structure of the Japanese language*. Cambridge, MA.: MIT Press.
Kuno, Susumu. 1978. *Danwa no bunpoo* [Grammar of Discourse]. Tokyo: Taishukan.
Kuno, Susumu. 1986. Anaphora in Japanese. In *Working Papers from the First SDF Workshop in Japanese Syntax*, ed. Shige-Yuki Kuroda, 11–70. La Jolla, CA: Department of Linguistics, University of California, San Diego.
Kuno, Susumu. 1987. *Functional syntax: Anaphora, discourse and empathy*. Chicago: University of Chicago Press.
Kuno, Susumu. 2004. Empathy and direct discourse perspectives. In *The handbook of pragmatics*, eds. Laurence R. Horn and Gregory Ward, 315–343. Oxford: Blackwell.
Kuroda, Shige-Yuki. 1965. *Generative grammatical studies in the Japanese language*. Ph.D. dissertation, Massachusetts Institute of Technology.
Kuroda, Shige-Yuki. 1973. On Kuno's direct discourse analysis of the Japanese reflexive *zibun*. *Papers in Japanese Linguistics* 2: 136–47.
Kutsch Lojenga, Constance. 1994. *Ngiti: A Central-Sudanic language of Zaire*. Köln: Rüdiger Köppe Verlag.
Lakoff, George. 1968. *Deep and surface grammar*. Bloomington, Indiana: Indiana University Linguistics Club.
Lasnik, Howard. 1976. Remarks on coreference. *Linguistic Analysis* 2: 1–22.
Lasnik, Howard. 1989. On the necessity of binding conditions. In *Essays on anaphora*, ed. Howard Lasnik, 149–167. Dordrecht: Kluwer.
Lasnik, Howard. 2001. Subjects, objects, and the EPP. In *Objects and other subjects: Grammatical functions, functional categories, and configurationality*, eds. William D. Davies and Stanley Dubinsky, 103–121. Dordrecht: Kluwer.
Lasnik, Howard, and Mamoru Saito. 1991. On the subject of infinitives. In *Papers from the 27th Regional Meeting of the Chicago Linguistic Society*, eds. Lise Dobrin, Lynn Nichols, and Rosa Rodriduez, 324–343. Chicago: Chicago Linguistic Society.
Lebeaux, David. 1983. A distributional difference between reciprocals and reflexives. *Linguistic Inquiry* 14: 723–730.
Lebeaux, David. 1984. Locality and anaphoric binding. *The Linguistic Review* 4: 343–363.
Lebeaux, David. 1988. *Language acquisition and the form of grammar*. Ph.D. dissertation, University of Massachusetts, Amherst.
Levinson, Stephen. 1987. Pragmatics and the grammar of anaphora: A partial pragmatic reduction of Binding and Control phenomena, *Journal of Linguistics* 23:

379–434.
Liu, Chen-Sheng Luther. 2001. Antilogophoricity, sympathy and the sympathetic antilogophor *Renjia*. *Journal of East Asian Linguistics* 10: 307–336.
Liu, Chen-Sheng Luther. 2004. Antilogophoricity, epithets and the empty antilogophor in Chinese. *Journal of East Asian Linguistics* 13: 257–287.
Maling, Joan. 1984. Non-clause bounded reflexives in modern Icelandic. *Linguistics and Philosophy* 7: 211–241.
Manzini, M. Rita, and Kenneth Wexler. 1987. Parameters, binding theory and learnability. *Linguistic Inquiry* 18: 413–444.
Martin, Samuel. 1975. *A reference grammar of Japanese*. New Haven: Yale University Press.
McCray Alexa T. 1980. The semantics of backward anaphora. In *Proceedings of the 10th Annual Meeting of the North Eastern Linguistic Society*, ed. John Jensen, 329–343. Ottawa: University of Ottawa.
Montalbetti, Mario. 1984. *After binding: On the interpretation of pronouns*. Ph.D. dissertation, Massachusetts Institute of Technology.
Narahara, Tomiko. 1991. *Nominal categories and binding theory*. Ph.D. dissertation, Harvard University.
Nishigauchi, Taisuke. 1986. *Quantification in syntax*. Ph.D. dissertation, University of Massachusetts, Amherst.
Noguchi, Tohru. 1997. Two types of pronouns and variable binding. *Language* 73: 770–797.
O'Grady, William. 2005. *Syntactic carpentry: An emergentist approach to syntax*. Mahwah, NJ: Lawrence Erlbaum.
Oshima, David Yoshikazu. 2004. *Zibun* revisited: empathy, logophoricity, and binding. *University of Washington Working Papers in Linguistics* 23: 175–190.
Oshima, David Yoshikazu. 2006. *Perspectives in reported discourse*. Ph.D. dissertation, Stanford University.
Oshima, David Yoshikazu. 2007. On empathic and logophoric binding. *Research on Language and Computation* 5: 19–35.
Oshima, Shin. 1979. Conditions on rules: anaphora in Japanese. In *Explorations in linguistics: Papers in honor of Kazuko Inoue*, eds. Georges Bedel, Eichi Kobayashi and Masatake Muraki, 423–448. Tokyo: Kenkyusya.
Parker, Elizabeth. 1986. Mundani pronouns, In *Pronominal system*, ed. Ursula Wiesemann, 131–165. Tübingen: Narr.
Patel-Grosz, Pritty. 2012. *Anti-locality at the interfaces*. Ph.D. dissertation, Massachusetts Institute of Technology.
Pearl, Lisa, and Benjamin Mis. 2012. Induction problems, indirect positive evidence, and universal grammar: Anaphoric one revisited, ms., University of California, Irvine.
Pica, Pierre. 1987. On the nature of the reflexivization cycle. In *Proceedings of the North Eastern Linguistic Society* 17, eds. Joyce Mcdonough and Bernadette Plunkett, 483–499. Amherst, MA.: GLSA.

Pica, Pierre. 1994. Condition C and epistemic contexts: A case study of epithets and anti-logophoric pronouns in French. In *Explorations in generative grammar: A festschrift for Dong-Whee Yang*, eds. Young-Sun Kim, Byung-Choon Lee, Kyoung-Jae Lee, Kyun-Kwon Yang, and Jong-Kuri Yoon, 544–570. Seoul: Hankuk Publishing Co..

Pollard, Carl, and Ivan Sag. 1992. Anaphors in English and the scope of Binding Theory. *Linguistic Inquiry* 23: 261–303.

Pollard, Carl, and Ivan Sag. 1994. *Head-driven phrase structure grammar*. Chicago: University of Chicago Press.

Postal, Paul. 1974. *On raising: An inquiry into one rule of English grammar and its theoretical implications*. Cambridge, MA.: MIT Press.

Prince, Ellen F. 1981. Toward a taxonomy of given-new information, In *Radical pragmatics*, ed. Peter Cole, 223–255. New York: Academic Press.

Reinhart, Tanya. 1983. *Anaphora and semantic interpretation*. Chicago: University of Chicago Press.

Reinhart, Tanya. 2000. Strategies of anaphora resolution. In *Interface strategies*, eds. Hans Bennis, Martin Everaert and Eric Reuland, 295–325. Amsterdam: Royal Academy of Arts and Sciences.

Reinhart, Tanya. 2006. *Interface strategies: Optimal and costly computations*. Cambridge, MA.: MIT Press.

Reinhart, Tanya, and Eric Reuland. 1991. Anaphors and logophors: An argument structure perspective. In *Long-distance anaphora*, eds. Jan Koster and Eric Reuland, 283–321. Cambridge: Cambridge University Press.

Reinhart, Tanya, and Eric Reuland. 1993. Reflexivity. *Linguistic Inquiry* 24: 657–720.

Roelofsen, Floris. 2010. Condition B effects in two simple steps. *Natural Language Semantics* 18: 115–140.

Ross, John Robert. 1967. *Constraints on variables in syntax*. Ph.D. dissertation, Massachusetts Institute of Technology.

Ruwet, Nicolas. 1990. En et y: Deux clitiques pronominaux antilogophoriques. *Langages* 97: 51–81.

Safir, Ken. 2004a. *The syntax of anaphora*. Oxford: Oxford University Press.

Safir, Ken. 2004b. *The syntax of (in)dependence*. Cambridge, MA.: MIT Press.

Sag, Ivan. 1976. *Deletion and logical form*. Ph.D. dissertation, Massachusetts Institute of Technology.

Saito, Mamoru. 1992. Long distance scrambling in Japanese. *Journal of East Asian Linguistics* 1, 69–118.

Saito, Mamoru, and Hajime Hoji. 1983. Weak crossover and move α in Japanese. *Natural Language and Linguistic Theory* 1: 245–259.

Sansom, George. 1928. *An historical grammar of Japanese*. Oxford: Oxford University Press.

Schaub, Willi. 1985. *Babungo*. London: Croom Helm.

Schlenker, Philippe. 2003. Clausal equations (a note on the connectivity problem). *Natural Language and Linguistic Theory* 21: 157–214.

Schlenker, Philippe. 2005. Minimize restrictors! (Notes on definite descriptions, Condition C and epithets). In *Proceedings of Sinn und Bedeutung* 9, eds. Emar Maier, Corien Bary, and Janneke Huitink, 385–416. Nijmegen: Netherlands.

Sells, Peter. 1987a. Aspects of logophoricity. *Linguistic Inquiry* 18: 445–479.

Sells, Peter. 1987b. Backwards anaphora and discourse structure: Some considerations. *CSLI publications: Reports* 114, 1–27.

Shibata, Natsumi, and Jun Yashima. 2014. Reference-set computation in children: Mandarin-speaking children's pronoun interpretation in Avoid Pronoun contexts, *Language Acquisition* 21: 304–315.

Shibatani, Masayoshi. 1978. Mikami Akira and the notion of "subject" in Japanese grammar. In *Problems in Japanese syntax and semantics*, eds. John Hinds and Irwin Howard, 52–67. Tokyo: Kaitakusha.

Sportiche, Dominique. 1986. Zibun. *Linguistic Inquiry* 17: 369–374.

Stirling, Lesley. 1993. *Switch-reference and discourse representation*. Cambridge: Cambridge University Press.

Sundaresan, Sandhya. 2012. *Context and (co)reference in the syntax and its interfaces*. Ph.D. dissertation, University of Stuttgart and University of Tromsø.

Takubo, Yukinori. 1990. Daikusisu to danwakoozoo [Deixis and discourse structure]. In *Nihongo to nihongo kyooiku* 12, ed. Tatsuo Kondo, 127–147. Tokyo: Meiji Shoin.

Tomlin, Russell. 1987. Linguistic reflections of cognitive events. In *Coherence and grounding in discourse*, ed. Russell Tomlin, 455–479. Amsterdam: John Benjamins.

Tomlin, Russell, and Ming-Ming Pu. 1991. The management of reference in Mandarin discourse. *Cognitive Linguistics* 2: 65–95.

Ueyama, Ayumi. 1998. *Two types of dependency*. Ph.D. dissertation, University of Southern California [distributed by GSIL publications].

Van Hoek, Karen. 1995. Conceptual reference points: A cognitive grammar account of pronominal anaphora constraints. *Language* 71, 310–340.

Williams, Edwin. 1977. Discourse and logical form. *Linguistic Inquiry* 8, 101–139.

Williams, Edwin. 1985. PRO and subject of NP. *Natural Language and Linguistic Theory* 3, 297–315.

Yashima, Jun. 2015. On the apparent unbindability of overt third-person pronouns in Japanese. *Natural Language and Linguistic Theory* 33, 1421–1438.

Index

Author Index

A
Abe, Jun   35, 57, 59, 117, 119, 120
Abbott, Edwin Abbott   65
Anderson, Stephen   1
Aoun, Joseph   1, 7, 53, 56–59, 86, 89
Ariel, Mira   71, 80–81

B
Battistella, Edwin   2
Bolinger, Dwight   114
Bond, Oliver   27
Bruening, Benjamin   106
Büring, Daniel   112

C
Charnavel, Isabelle   4–5, 23, 116, 121
Chomsky, Noam   13–14, 18, 44, 58, 107–108
Choueiri, Lina   86, 89
Clements, George Nicholas   21, 24–26, 28–29, 31, 35–36
Collins, Chris   10, 98, 107

Comrie, Bernard   25, 27–28, 30, 35
Conroy, Stacey   49
Corazza, Eros   104
Culy, Christopher   26–27, 35, 116

D
Déchaine, Rose-Marie   7, 48, 52–53, 66–70, 101
Dorgeloh, Heidrun   135
Drummond, Alex   121
Dubinsky, Stanley   6, 8, 40–41, 87–90, 106, 111, 115, 135, 139

E
Elbourne, Paul   61, 70, 74
Emonds, Joseph   99
Evans, Gareth   74

F
Freidin, Robert   1

G
Givón, Talmy   71, 81
Green, Georgia M.   134–135

151

Greenberg, Joseph 62
Grinder, John T. 21
Grodzinsky, Yosef 5, 43–44, 50, 87, 105

H
Hagège, Claude 24–25, 32
Haïk, Isabelle 40, 90
Hamilton, Robert 6, 8, 40–41, 87–90, 106, 111, 115, 135, 139
Hara, Takaaki 7, 49, 75–76, 80–84, 93–94, 102–103
Heim, Irene 45, 112
Higginbotham, James 13, 60, 112
Hinds, John 71, 91,
Hoji, Hajime 7, 48–53, 55, 72–80, 93–94, 102
Hornstein, Norbert 1, 7, 53, 56–59, 85–86
Huang, C.-T. James 118–119
Huang, Yan 35
Hyman, Larry M. 25, 27–28, 30, 35

I
Inoue, Kazuko 36

J
Jackendoff, Ray 19, 84, 97
Jespersen, Otto 65
Jones, Ross 27, 30, 32–34

K
Kanzaki, Takaaki 50, 65
Kameyama, Megumi 2
Katada, Fusa 7, 36, 53, 56, 58–59
Kayne, Richard 86, 109
Keenan, Edward 42
Kishida, Maki 35, 117
Kitagawa, Chisato 36, 48, 52, 55, 72
Koopman, Hilda 4, 6
Kuno, Susumu 2–4, 6, 8, 27, 30, 36, 41, 87, 100, 104, 106, 114, 117–120, 125, 132
Kuroda, Shige-Yuki 62–67, 70, 119
Kutsch Lojenga, Constance 34–35

L
Lakoff, George 106
Lasnik, Howard 2, 13–14, 57, 85–87, 103
Lebeaux, David 19, 58, 108
Levinson, Stephen 71
Liu, Chen-Sheng Luther 6, 118–119

M
Maling, Joan 2
Manzini, M. Rita 1
Martin, Samuel 66, 72
McCray Alexa T. 133, 135
Mis Benjamin 48
Montalbetti, Mario 7, 53, 60–61

N
Narahara, Tomiko 2, 6, 8, 40–41, 87–88, 90, 106
Nishigauchi, Taisuke 74
Noguchi, Tohru 7, 48, 52–53, 57, 61, 64–67, 70–71, 73–74, 91, 101

O
O'Grady, William 129–131
Oshima, David Yoshikazu 35, 116–117, 119
Oshima, Shin 120

P
Parker, Elizabeth 32
Patel-Grosz, Pritty 6, 88–89, 98–99
Pearl, Lisa 48
Pica, Pierre 2, 6, 87
Pollard, Carl 2, 4, 19–22, 121, 142
Postal, Paul 10, 85, 97–98
Pu, Ming-Ming 80
Prince, Ellen F 81

R
Reinhart, Tanya 2, 4–5, 20, 43–45, 50, 87, 105, 108–109, 116, 121
Reuland, Eric 2, 4, 20, 116, 121
Roelofsen, Floris 44–45
Ross, John Robert 99

Ruwet, Nicolas 6
S
Safir, Ken 20, 86, 110, 112, 115
Sag, Ivan 2, 4, 19–22, 42, 121, 142
Saito, Mamoru 48, 51–52, 55, 57, 85–86
Sansom, George 72
Schaub, Willi 28
Schlenker, Philippe 109, 112
Sells, Peter 2–4, 6, 8, 30, 35, 37–39, 89, 106, 111–117, 119, 124–125, 127, 133–135, 139
Shibata, Natsumi 49
Shibatani, Masayoshi 36
Sportiche, Dominique 4–7, 23, 48, 52–53, 55, 57, 121
Stirling, Lesley 26, 32, 35

Sundaresan, Sandhya 4
T
Takubo, Yukinori 92
Tomlin, Russell 80
U
Ueyama, Ayumi 74, 76–78
V
Van Hoek, Karen 106
W
Weinberg, Amy 85
Wexler, Kenneth 1
Williams, Edwin 42, 107
Wiltschko, Martina 7, 48, 52–53, 66–70, 101
Y
Yashima, Jun 49

Subject Index

A

A'-free 56–59
A'-movement 57, 59
A'-position 56, 58–59
accessibility 80–84, 103
accessibility marking scale 81
Accessibility Theory 80
A-free 56, 87
A-movement 108
anaphor 2–5, 9–23, 49, 53–56, 58, 62, 81, 88, 117, 119–121, 142
  exempt 5, 20–23, 142
  long-distance 2–4, 121
  operator 58
  plain/non-exempt 5, 20, 22–23
anti-locality 54–57, 89
antilogophor 40, 112, 140
antilogophoric effect 6–7, 24, 90, 96, 99–101, 106, 110–111, 124, 131, 136, 139–140
antilogophoricity constraint/restriction 6, 8, 24, 41, 84, 87–91, 93–101, 106–107, 109–112, 115, 122–125, 129, 132, 135–137, 140, 142
A-position 56, 59, 85–86
appositive 8, 97–99, 101, 140
attitude report 93
attitude verb 96
Avoid Pronoun Principle 49
awareness 3, 117–121 See also point of view, consciousness, perspective

B

binding 1–9, 12–15, 18–20, 22–24, 35, 39, 41–45, 47–50, 55–57, 61–62, 66–68, 72, 76, 78–80, 82–87, 92, 95, 97–98, 101, 103, 105, 108–109, 112–113, 117, 120, 122–127, 129, 137, 140
A-binding/A-bind/A-bound 1, 44, 86–87
A'-binding/A'-bind/A'-bound 1, 56–57, 85–86
local binding/locally bound 2, 35, 47, 55, 59, 68, 117, 119–120
logophoric 4, 117, 123, 125–126, 129, 137
non-local 47
pronominal 47–48, 56
quantificational 95
semantic 43, 97
structural 4, 6, 23, 35, 103
variable 5, 7, 41, 43, 45, 50, 55, 85, 87, 98, 105, 108–109
Babungo 28
binding domain 1–2, 20
Binding Theory 1–2, 5–9, 12–14, 18–20, 22–23, 43–44, 47–48, 67, 105, 112
Boko 27, 30, 32–34, 117

C

c-command 2–3, 5–6, 8, 12–14, 16, 18–20, 43, 50, 54, 56–57, 59, 77, 85–86, 90, 94, 105–110, 124, 130, 132
coargument-based theory 20, 22–23
coindexation/coindexing 13–14, 20, 48, 89–90, 111, 126
common noun 62–65, 69–70, 72
complete functional complex (CFC) 14–17, 20, 56
Condition A 2, 5, 12–16, 20, 22–23, 121
Condition B 1, 5, 8, 12, 14, 16–17, 24, 43–45, 49, 67–69, 72, 84, 87–91, 93–95, 98, 101, 110, 140
Condition C 2, 5, 8, 12, 14, 17–18, 24, 67, 69, 86–88, 90, 105–112, 115,

122–125, 129–130, 132–133, 136–137, 140–141
consciousness 3, 23, 110, 118. *See also* point of view, awareness, perspective
coreference 7, 11, 25, 34, 41–45, 47–48, 50, 52, 58, 68, 73, 87, 97, 99, 112, 114, 124, 130, 136–137, 141
   accidental 11, 44, 50
   intended/presupposed 44, 112
   intrasentential 44–45
covaluation 41, 45

D
de dicto 89
demonstrative 70–75, 81, 84, 92, 100, 142
   a-series 72–73
   ko-series 72–73
   so-series 72–74
de se 119
D-indexed 77–78
direct speech 39
discourse role 37, 113–115, 133
domino effect 32

E
economy 44, 50, 58, 71
Eleme 27
ellipsis 42
empathy 104, 114, 116
epithet 8, 40, 84–92, 96–101, 104–106, 110–111, 139–140, 142
   anaphoric 97
   appositive 8, 97, 101, 140
Ewe 25–26, 28, 31, 35–36
experiencer 26, 87, 126

F
focus particle 42
Formal Dependency (FD) 77–78

G
Gokana 25, 27–28, 30

I
Icelandic 2–4, 39
I-indexed 77–78
Inclusiveness Condition 13
Indexical Dependency (ID) 77
indirect discourse 37–38, 94, 111. *See also* reported speech
intervention effect 21–22, 125–127, 142

J
Japanese 2–4, 7–8, 26–27, 29–30, 33–36, 38–39, 47–57, 60–76, 78, 80–81, 83–84, 91–93, 95–101, 103–104, 113, 117–118, 121–123, 125–126, 129, 137, 140

L
learnability 48
LF 2, 44, 56–61, 77, 85, 107
local antecedent 18, 44–45, 87–89, 119
local domain 12, 14–17, 69, 110
logocentric antecedent 24, 31, 35, 37, 39, 111–114, 116–117, 127, 136, 139
logocentric argument 132
logocentric NP 87
logocentric predicate 32
logocentric verb hierarchy 26
logophor 5, 23–25, 32, 35–37, 39, 116–117, 119, 121
logophoric binding *See* binding
logophoric center 40, 99, 107–108, 110, 114–115, 122–124
logophoric complement 87
logophoric domain 24–27, 29, 31–33, 35, 39, 112, 115, 131–132, 140
logophoric effect 32, 111, 129, 133
logophoric form 26, 31, 33, 35, 116
logophoric pronoun 2–3, 20, 24–26, 28, 31–34, 36, 111, 115–117, 140
logophoric verb 37, 87

M
Mundang 25, 32

Mundani 31–32
N
Ngiti 34–35, 117
O
Overt Pronoun Constraint (OPC) 60–61
P
perspective 20–21, 23, 29, 38, 40, 88–89, 100, 109–110, 116, 121. *See also* point of view, awareness, consciousness
φ-feature 67, 69, 70
PIVOT 37–39, 111, 113–117, 127–129, 131–136, 139–140
point of view 3, 20, 23, 28, 37–38, 40, 113–114, 116, 118–119, 133
possessive 33–34, 109
possessor 33–34, 84, 108–109
pronoun 1–3, 5, 7–8, 10–12, 14, 16–18, 20, 24–26, 28–29, 31–35, 41–45, 47–58, 60–72, 75–88, 90–93, 95–107, 109–111, 115–118, 122, 124, 130–135, 140
   antilogophoric 8, 87, 96, 99, 106, 110
   bound 7, 45, 50, 52, 54, 76, 80, 96
   referential 10, 45, 50–51, 55, 66, 78, 99
   D- 66, 101
   E-type 77–78
   first-person 63
   logophoric *See* logophoric pronoun
   N- 66, 70, 101
   null/zero 8, 29, 53, 58, 60, 66, 81–83, 97–98, 100, 140
   third-person 7–8, 47–50, 52–55, 57–58, 61–63, 65–68, 70–72, 75–76, 78, 80, 82–84, 91–93, 95–96, 101, 103–104
   possessive 34
   second-person 63
purpose clause 27–29

Q
quantificational/quantified antecedent 43, 50, 86, 93, 98
Quantifier Raising (QR) 56, 60, 85
R
reciprocal 12, 19
reconstruction 57, 78–79, 107–108
referential antecedent 50, 52
referential dependency 9–10, 13–14, 79
reflexive 2, 4–5, 12, 18–23, 25, 29, 36, 53–54, 57, 81, 103, 116
   long-distance 25, 116
   picture-noun 4–5, 21–22
relative clause 27, 31–33, 63, 70, 79, 97, 126, 132
reported speech 25, 27, 40. *See also* indirect discourse
reported speaker *See* speaker
R-expression 7–8, 11–12, 14, 17–18, 62, 67, 86–88, 105–107, 109–110, 114–115, 124, 130, 135, 142
Rule I 5, 44–45, 50, 87, 105
S
scrambling 57
SELF 37–39, 89–90, 94, 100, 111, 113–114, 116–117, 127–129, 134–135, 139
sloppy reading/interpretation 42, 51–52, 95, 100–101
SOURCE 37–39, 89–90, 94, 100, 111, 113–115, 117, 127–129, 131–136, 139–140
speaker 4, 24, 28–29, 37–39, 45, 72–73, 77, 80, 89, 91, 99–100, 104, 109, 116, 120, 130, 132–136
   current speaker 37, 89, 134–136. *See also* external speaker
   external speaker 28–29, 37–39, 89, 100, 132. *See also* current speaker
   internal speaker 29. *See also* reported speaker

reported speaker 89, 116. *See also* internal speaker
strict reading/interpretation 42, 52, 95, 100
subject orientation 35
Super Equi 21
supreme intervention configuration 129, 135, 140

T
3POV 37–38

V
variable 5, 7–8, 41–45, 48–50, 52–57, 60–61, 66–67, 74–80, 82–85, 87–88, 91, 93–95, 98, 101–102, 105, 108–109
bound 7–8, 42–45, 48–49, 52–55, 61, 66–67, 74–80, 83–85, 91, 93–95, 98, 101–102
formal 60–61
free 42, 77

W
weak crossover 57

Z
0-indexed 77–80

Antilogophoricity and Binding Theory

著作者　八島　純

発行者　武村哲司

2016年11月19日　第1版第1刷発行©

発行所　株式会社　開拓社　　〒113-0023 東京都文京区向丘1-5-2
電話　(03)5842-8900（代表）
振替　00160-8-39587
http://www.kaitakusha.co.jp

印刷　株式会社　あるむ　　ISBN978-4-7589-2233-3　C3080